THE CONFESSION

THE CONFESSION
Interrogation and Criminal Profiles
for Police Officers

By John M. Macdonald, M.D. *Marshall* , *1920 –*

Professor of Psychiatry and
Director of Forensic Psychiatry
University of Colorado Health Sciences Center
Denver, Colorado

and

Lieutenant David L. Michaud
Crimes Against Persons Bureau
Denver Police Department

Apache Press
Denver, Colorado

Published and distributed by
Apache Press
P.O. Box 6526
Denver, Colorado 80206

International Standard Book Number 0-9618230-0-3
Library of Congress Catalog Card Number 87-70690
© 1987 by John Macdonald. All rights reserved.
Printed in the United States of America

CONTENTS

ACKNOWLEDGMENTS

Police officers from many law enforcement agencies have helped us write this book. We are grateful for their advice. The following detectives of the Denver Police Department contributed their expertise: Dale Burkhart and David Martin on armed robbery; Michael Staskin on burglary; Robert A. Thiede on check offenses; Dennis Cribari, Larry Subia and Marcus Vasquez on drug offenses; Daril Cinquanta on informants; as well as James Burkhalter and David Haley on bombings.

Police Chief Thomas E. Coogan gave encouragement and supported preparation of this manual. Investigation Division Chiefs Casey Simpson and Donald B. Mulnix, together with Captain James J. Fitzpatrick were all most helpful. Captain James D. Persichitte and Lieutenant J.V. Sarconi of the Denver Fire Department gave assistance on arson. Craig L. Truman provided legal advice.

We have drawn upon the criminal profiling research of the Behavioral Science Unit and upon the hostage negotiation research of the Special Operations and Research Unit of the FBI Academy, but the information provided on these subjects does not represent the viewpoint of the FBI, and no such claim is made.

This is the fifth book that Mrs. Carolyn Zwibecker has typed for John. Her cheerful personality, her skill and her willingness to help at all times are greatly appreciated.

Ed Stein designed the book and its cover. Brad Thompson edited the manuscript and read the proofs. David Cornwell took the cover photos.

PREFACE

Quite simply, this is a practical guide to criminal interrogation, the questioning of witnesses and the usefulness of criminal profiles.

It is intended for patrolmen and patrolwomen, for recently promoted detectives, and for detectives in smaller police departments who may be called on at any time to investigate crimes that they seldom encounter. Although it was not intended for experienced investigators, we have been gratified by the positive response of seasoned detectives, who were asked to read chapters and suggest improvements. They felt that quite a few of their colleagues could benefit from reading it.

This is not a textbook on the law governing criminal interrogations. The law changes, and the law varies from one jurisdiction to another. Readers who have any question should seek legal advice.

In this book we do not repeat he or she every time we refer to a police officer, a victim, a witness or a suspect. This is to save space and make the book more readable.

Chapter 1

INTRODUCTION TO CRIMINAL INTERROGATION

Questioning is not a mode of conversation among gentlemen.

Samuel Johnson, Boswell, *Life*, 1776

Criminal interrogation is defined as the formal questioning of a criminal suspect. It is a strong term. Some police departments prefer to talk of interviewing suspects. Perhaps they are fearful that the term criminal interrogation will conjure up in the minds of citizens and defense attorneys the prolonged, forceful questioning under bright lights of a suspect who has been denied sleep, nourishment and legal advice. Present-day detectives do not use such techniques, and no courts would tolerate such abuse.

The advantage of the term criminal interrogation over the word interviewing is that it implies a much more active role on the part of the detective. Interrogation is often hard work that requires careful preparation, keen observation and persistence. Some police officers seem to have a way with words, a way with people and an inborn gift that enables them to obtain sensitive information. All police officers can improve their technique, and that is the purpose of this book, to provide practical advice on criminal interrogation.

The questioning of victims and witnesses can be just as important as the interrogation of suspects. Indeed, in some cases identification of the offender may be dependent upon skillful questioning of a bystander. Yet often at a major crime scene with many possible witnesses at the scene, patrolmen may perform this task. Among the officers, there may be one who has just graduated from the training academy, yet police training academies do not always provide sufficient instruction on the art of obtaining information from citizens. Many of the techniques of criminal interrogation are of value in questioning victims and witnesses, but in general the approach is gentler.

Quick assessment of the personality of a suspect, victim or witness is a valuable aid to successful questioning. The interrogator has to be familiar with the features of the crime under investigation. This is not a problem in large police departments where detectives specialize in the investigation of such crimes as homicide, assault, armed robbery, sex offenses, burglary, drug and vice offenses. Small police departments do not have the luxury of detectives who specialize.

One detective may have to investigate all felonies. He may have to question a child molester one day, an arsonist the next week and an armed robber the following week. He does not have day-to-day familiarity with these crimes, yet he needs to know the essential questions that he should ask a suspect. Textbooks describe these crimes at length, but seldom list routine questions that might be of value. Criminal profiles of murderers, rapists, arsonists and other offenders will be provided to help police officers know the questions to ask and how to ask them.

THE COMPULSION TO CONFESS

My conscience has a thousand several tongues, and every tongue brings in a several tale and every tale condemns me for a villain.

Shakespeare, *Richard III*

Some criminals, while making every effort to avoid detection, nevertheless seem compelled to betray themselves. Their consciences allow them to commit the crimes, yet seem to make them behave in such a manner that they will be caught and punished. At the crime scene they make simple blunders that make their arrest likely, if not inevitable. For example, a safecracker leaves his jacket in the bank. His parole papers are in a pocket. A thief, who is a watchmaker, alters nine out of 10 stolen watches so that they cannot be identified, then pawns the only watch he has not altered.

It might be argued that such simple mistakes are made by criminals who are tired or under the influence of alcohol or drugs. This is not always so. The kidnapper and murderer of Adolph Coors III, a wealthy Colorado brewer, planned his crime carefully, but in checking the rural area where he intended to kidnap his victim, he used his distinctive car, a yellow Mercury. A citizen later remembered seeing this car parked near his home. A check of motor vehicle registrations showed there were only five yellow Mercury cars registered in the Denver area. Clues have been well described as the traces of guilt that the criminal leaves behind him.

The criminal with a compulsion to confess talks too much. For example, Ed Gein, the grave robber and murderer of Plainfield, Wisconsin, told a group of local citizens discussing the disappearance of Mary Hogan, a tavern keeper in a nearby town, "She's up at the house now." This comment was passed off as a joke. Two years later her body was found hanging from the ceiling of Ed Gein's home dressed like a deer, with the head severed from the body.

Under interrogation, the criminal with a compulsion to confess, while denying the crime, may say things that were better left unsaid.

The alert interrogator will recognize the significance of some remark that seems unrelated to the crime, as in the following example:

A 36 year-old man and his common-law wife were arrested after they cashed checks belonging to a rich bachelor who had been missing for several weeks. The couple claimed that the missing man, before going on a trip to New Mexico, had given them permission to cash the checks and to live in his Denver home. Murder was suspected, but the body could not be located. When the suspects were questioned, they mentioned repeatedly the name of a friend. When the friend was interviewed, she volunteered that she had spent an afternoon with the couple at a picnic ground in the mountains. She recalled that her host had shown unusual interest in a pile of rocks. Police investigation of the picnic site led to the discovery of the burial site beneath the rock pile.

WHY CRIMINALS CONFESS

> *The secrets of life are not shown except to sympathy and likeness.*
> Emerson, *Representative Men: Montaigne*

Not all criminals have a compulsion to confess, and even those with this compulsion may remain silent. Skillful interrogation is the most important stimulus for confession. Even a career criminal who says only, "If you've got it, file it." may later confess to a persistent, skillful interrogator. Criminal offenders confess when they are tired, off balance, ill at ease, when they are distracted by unexpected kindness or surprised by a harsh unforgiving approach.

They may have to tell someone what they have just done, even if the only available person is a police officer. They may speak when they feel justified in committing the crime, ("It was the victim's fault; he shouldn't have said that to me.") or when they need the approval of the questioner. Anxiety, despair and vanity are among other reasons for confession.

Some criminals confess when they are caught in the act. They feel that all is lost and reveal their guilt, providing some slight effort is made at the time of their arrest to obtain a confession. The burglar, discovered late at night with eight new microwave ovens in his station wagon near a warehouse that has been broken into, may feel discouraged and ready to admit his crime. If the patrolmen tell him that the burglary detective will talk to him, this may not occur until the next day. If he is not questioned immediately he will not be so vulnerable later as his self-confidence will be restored overnight. Other inmates, all skillful jailhouse lawyers, tell him to remain silent and suggest a number of plausible explanations for the presence of the microwave ovens.

The armed robber confronted with overwhelming evidence, for example a clear picture of him with a gun in his hand taken by a hidden camera in a convenience store, may feel that it will be to his advantage to confess to some robberies in plea bargaining. Naturally, he will confess only to those robberies in which no one was hurt.

Unbearable feelings of guilt lead to confession. A murderer may walk into a police station and tell the officer on duty that five years earlier he killed a prostitute.

Curiosity and an ill-timed remark tripped one thief. A man arrested in the act of stealing from a trailer hauling an interstate shipment denied any knowledge of the theft and refused to admit his guilt. After the interview, the FBI agents carried out the cartons that had been stolen and in doing so passed in front of the suspect who absent-mindedly called out, "Can I see what I stole?" The cartons contained stove and refrigerator parts.

A criminal may confess felonies in the hope of avoiding conviction of a more serious crime. A man arrested on suspicion of murder, although a career criminal who ordinarily would not admit to any crime, quickly confessed to a series of burglaries. "I don't know what you guys are trying to put on me, I'm a burglar, I'll admit that, but I ain't no killer."

There was insufficient evidence to convict him of the murders of two young men, and it was considered that he confessed to the burglaries to forestall a full-scale investigation of the murders.

The occasional young offender who wants to establish a reputation may confess to a crime that he has committed because he wants the status of a penitentiary sentence. Other, less common reasons for confession include the desire to join a dominant homosexual lover in prison ("Put me in the same cell as that motherfucker, I love him."); a need to bring shame on one's parents through a criminal conviction; to cause the arrest and conviction of a disliked accomplice; or to secure the release from custody of a girlfriend who also was involved in the crime.

A criminal who receives only a short sentence after making a full confession mistakenly may think he will get the same consideration from the court the next time he is arrested, if once again he makes a full confession. A good deal the first time is no guarantee of a good deal the second time. A man facing a long prison sentence in a state with a harsh penal system may confess to crimes he has committed in a state where the penitentiary has a higher standard of living.

The motives for confession may lie in the detective-suspect relationship. There can be a battle of wills in which a grudging respect for the officer may be decisive. There may even be a desire for friendship, a need for sympathy, understanding or forgiveness. The emotional interplay between the two may change during the questioning, and neither person may be fully aware of the progressive changes in the relationship, but when it is all over there may be a bond that neither acknowledges, which may be hidden behind words of disrespect or even personal abuse.

Suspects may retract their confessions before trial, and courts with distressing frequency exclude confessions from evidence, often for questionable reasons. Videotaping confessions may help persuade courts that a suspect's claims of undue coercion, for example, lack basis. Society, if not courts of law, attach great importance to confessions by criminal suspects. Theodore Reik points out in *The Compulsion to Confess* that "Confession is, indeed, the criminal's first step on his way back to society ... the criminal shows in his confession his intention to re-enter society by declaring himself deserving of punishment. The outsider is on his painful detour back to the family of man."

False Confessions

False confessions are a problem in major unsolved crimes that have attracted nationwide publicity. More than 200 people falsely confessed to the kidnapping and murder of Charles Lindberg's baby. The so-called "Black Dahlia" murder case in Los Angeles has not been solved, but more than 30 people have confessed to the mutilation-murder of fast-living Elizabeth Short. She was called the Black Dahlia because of her fondness for black dresses and black underclothing.

A wish for publicity and notoriety underlies many of these confessions. A few people who make false confessions of murder later commit murder. Other reasons for false confessions are to obtain a bed for the night in freezing weather, or to obtain transport to a distant city where the crime occurred. Two jail inmates in San Francisco sought out reporters to confess murdering several young women in Oregon and Washington. The men later admitted they made up the murder story from news reports of the Green River slayings of 26 young women in the Seattle area. They hoped they would be taken to Washington to look for bodies of women they claimed to have killed. Once in the woods, they thought they might be able to escape.

Forceful prolonged questioning with threats of violence is another factor. The story is told that SS leader Heinrich Himmler lost his pipe while visiting a concentration camp. A search followed, but on returning to his car he discovered it on his seat. "But sir," protested the camp commandant, "six prisoners have already confessed to stealing it." Criminals serving or facing long prison sentences will confess to murders they have not committed in a search for publicity, to obtain the release of other prisoners convicted of the murders or to cause trouble for district attorneys and law enforcement officers.

THE SKILLFUL INTERROGATOR

I have six honest serving-men
(They taught me all I knew):
Their names are What and Why and When
And How and Where and Who.
                    Rudyard Kipling, *The Serving-Men*

An authority once said of the good interrogator, "Essentially you have to like people; suspects and witnesses are like animals, they know, they have instincts." Certainly many experts meet this qualification, but there are many good interviewers who are by no means well-disposed toward their fellow men, least of all toward criminals. There are other essential qualities. It is difficult to list them in order of importance, but the ability to listen must come high on the list. It is easy to ask questions; it is difficult to remain silent.

The art of listening is very subtle: one has to listen attentively. An apparently trivial detail may not be irrelevant, it may be the key to the puzzle. Above all one has to be willing to listen, yet know when to cut short the talkative offender who is avoiding the issue. Clearly the interrogator should be confident. Confidence comes from experience and knowledge, including knowledge of the crime under investigation. But one should not be overconfident as suspects react negatively to interrogators who are obviously pleased with themselves.

Knowledge of interviewing techniques by itself is not enough. One has to be flexible in the use of these techniques. The ability to make a quick assessment of the suspect's personality is an advantage. The officer must have a high level of suspicion, so that he is quick to pick up statements that do not make sense. He should feel his way slowly, but be prepared to act swiftly if necessary. Throughout, he has to be very alert, watching not only for inconsistent statements, but also for nonverbal communication, for example changes in posture and movement, which may contradict the suspect's statements. He must be prepared to spend long hours at his work and be willing to cancel a dinner engagement at short notice. The good interrogator would probably earn far more money as a stockbroker or computer salesman, but his life would be much less exciting.

Chapter 2
QUESTIONING
THE SUSPECT

Silent people are dangerous.

La Fontaine, *Fables*

PREPARATION

Whenever possible before interviewing a suspect, the detective should review all available information on the crime under investigation and on the suspect. The detective should check the suspect's criminal record and computer records of contacts, which usually give the date, location and reason for a police stop, as well as information on the suspect's vehicle, home address, place of employment and names and addresses of his companions. *If it is a major case, and if time is available,* as for example when an arrest warrant has been issued but the suspect cannot be located, then information should be obtained not only from police officers who know the suspect, but from associates, confidential informants, employers and even members of his family.

These more detailed inquiries may provide vital information. For example, a man suspected of rape had an arrest 10 years previously for impersonating a police officer. A telephone call to the arresting officer revealed that the suspect posing as a detective had attempted to persuade a young woman to enter his car. A number of rapes in the same neighborhood had been committed by a man resembling the suspect and claiming to be a police officer. There was insufficient evidence to arrest him for these rapes.

Family members concerned about a suspect's potential for violence may willingly provide information. Family members concerned only to protect the suspect from arrest, may unwittingly let slip information, perhaps unrelated to the crime itself, that contributes to the detective's insight into the suspect's character. Estranged spouses and disgruntled lovers can be unusually helpful.

Good knowledge of a suspect's background can be used at a critical stage, the first interview. A skyjacker who parachuted from a United Air Lines jet plane with a large sum of money claimed amnesia and said that if he did commit this crime he must have been out of his mind as he had a fear of heights and his only previous air flights had been to and from Vietnam. After he was shown a copy of his army discharge papers, which listed him as a qualified helicopter air gunner, his memory improved.

When a great deal is known about the subject, and this is often the case when there are several prior arrests, arrange a strategic planning session. Decisions can be made on the method of interrogation and choice of interrogator, perhaps a detective who knows the suspect. Quick massive confrontation was successful in the case of a young man who was suspected of raping and killing an elderly woman and then setting fire to her home. When the firemen were shoveling ashes and debris out of the home, a policewoman noticed a plastic envelope containing this young man's identification papers, and a short time later he was arrested in the crawlspace of his parents' home alongside his victim's TV set.

A career burglar suddenly became involved in rapes with violence and the brutal stabbing of both male and female victims encountered in burglaries. A decision was made to approach him directly and immediately about this change in his behavior. An experienced detective sergeant was not discouraged by his initial response after his arrest, "Fuck you pigs, I'm not going to talk." The sergeant told him, "I remember you from District Three (police district). Joe, something happened to you, you're not a violent person, not a bad guy, you weren't like this when you were a burglar. What happened to you? Is there something wrong?" The suspect's head went down and he replied, "I don't know, something just snapped. I stomped her like a bug."

LOCATION

The ideal location for questioning is on your own turf, in your building. You are in familiar surroundings, this is your country, and you are at ease. The suspect in his home or office has an advantage over you. He has control of the environment. An exception to this rule occurs immediately after commission of the crime, when the suspect indicates that he is willing to talk. A statement can be taken at the scene and expanded on at police headquarters.

Another exception to this rule occurs when the interviewer wants to see the suspect in his own environment. The object is not to obtain a confession, but to obtain information and learn more about the suspect from his surroundings. The posters or pictures on the wall, the books in his bookcase, the envelopes or bills on his table and the people in his home can be taken in at a glance.

John had to interview—on the order of a federal judge—a number of prisoners in the maximum security cell block of a state penitentiary. Instead of seeing them in the prison hospital as had been arranged he insisted on seeing each man in his own cell. Curiously, the only prisoners who did not keep their cells scrupulously clean were prison informers. In addition to learning more about the prisoners from their cells, there was an unexpected advantage. John was seen as being macho because he ventured into "max" and this improved rapport with the prisoners.

PRIVACY

Confession is often difficult, and one should not add to the criminal's burden by asking him to reveal himself in the presence of several people. Ideally, there should only be one or two interrogators in the interviewing room with the suspect.

Privacy can be obtained in almost any situation. If one talks to a suspect on the street, his mind may be intent on creating a tough guy image for the benefit of bystanders. In the police car his words cannot be heard by spectators, he is no longer tempted to play to the gallery, and he can now concentrate on explaining his crime.

The need for privacy should require no emphasis, but it is surprising how often this rule is neglected. Perhaps the questioner feels that the suspect has no intention of talking anyway or that a confession is not needed as there is sufficient evidence to secure a conviction.

Yet one never knows if a suspect will talk, revealing information on other crimes, or whether other evidence will be sufficient for a successful prosecution. One should always attempt to obtain a confession no matter how difficult this may appear and no matter how trivial the offense. There are exceptions to the rule of the need for privacy. It may be more important for a questioner to seize the right moment to obtain a confession, for example, rather than risk losing it by delaying questioning until privacy can be assured, as in the following example.

A young man charged with shooting a police officer admitted to committing only those burglaries for which he had been convicted in court. John pointed out that most burglars commit 50 to 100 or more burglaries for every one they are charged with in court, and that he had to feed his heroin habit. However, he persisted in his denial of other burglaries. After completing a psychiatric evaluation, John was taking him back to his cell when a policewoman passed in the corridor.

This was the first time John had seen a policewoman in this small city, and he drew the suspect's attention to the young woman. He suddenly became very friendly, his eyes lit up and he commented that John must have been a tiger when he was young. It was obvious that he had assumed that John's interest in the policewoman was of a sexual nature. John seized the moment of friendliness to question the suspect about his burglaries. It was awkward standing and writing notes in the busy, narrow corridor, but the opportunity for obtaining this information might have been lost if John had taken the suspect back to the interviewing room.

THE INTERVIEWING ROOM

Questioning requires concentration on the part of interrogator and suspect. The latter welcomes any distraction that will take his mind off the painful subject under discussion. The suspect prefers a room with large windows or glass partitions that enable him to watch police department employees at work. The interrogator is so intent on his task and so familiar with his surroundings that he does not appreciate the interest the suspect has in framed diplomas, textbooks, pictures taken by a concealed camera of an armed robber holding up a bank clerk, mug shots and so on.

This point is illustrated by the case of John Gilbert Graham, the airplane bomber who caused the deaths of 44 people. There was a risk that his confession following prolonged interrogation might not be admitted in evidence. To determine his state of mind at the time of his confession John questioned him about the interviewing room. He described pictures on the wall of World War II Nazi saboteurs and of the history of fingerprinting. The interrogator confirmed only the presence of the pictures of the saboteurs. On checking the room John found that Graham's recall of the room was better than the interrogator's, as there was also the picture on the history of fingerprinting. The interrogator probably was concentrating on Graham and the plane bombing, whereas Graham was probably doing all he could to think of anything but hotshot batteries, timers and sticks of dynamite.

Some terrorist groups instruct their members on resistance to police questioning. For example, they are taught to concentrate on an object in the interrogation room. One terrorist, at his trial, claimed that the police had forced him to remember a six-digit number. The police were puzzled by this, and on checking they discovered a file on the interrogating officer's desk had this number, which the suspect seized upon as a way of distracting his attention from his interview.

The ideal interviewing room is simple, with bare walls, a desk or table and chairs. The chair for the suspect should be just as comfortable as the interrogator's chair. The suspect should sit alongside the desk so that the desk does not come between the participants. There should be no telephone, no police radio and no telephone beeper in the room. A flashing red light outside the door or a notice on the door "Interview in Progress" should prevent interruption of the interview. If a partner participates, make sure he is not wearing a telephone beeper.

MEETING THE SUSPECT

There are advantages in matching your appearance and manner to the personality of the suspect. A detective about to question the vice president of a corporation, a dentist or other professional may find it helpful to dress conservatively.

Some detectives dress formally at all times and their manner may match their clothing. Others are more casual, they may take off their sportscoat, roll up their sleeves, loosen their tie and approach the suspect in a relaxed manner, at least initially. Most detectives introduce themselves by rank and name. Before questioning begins the suspect must be advised of his rights.

THE MIRANDA WARNINGS

The art of beginning an interview with a suspect is to ensure that he does not remain silent when he is informed of his rights.

Paul Softley, *Police Interrogation*

Inbau, Reid and Buckley suggest in *Criminal Interrogation and Confession* that once the Miranda warnings have been given, followed by a waiver of rights, they should not be repeated unless there has been a considerable lapse of time since they were originally issued, for example, after a day or more. John Hinckley, the man who shot President Ronald Reagan, was given three Miranda warnings within two hours. After the third warning he requested an attorney. Craig Truman, a respected defense attorney, suggests that when interrogation is taken over by another police department or another law enforcement agency, the detective, who advised the suspect of his Miranda rights, should remain with him during any further interrogation.

Do not make a big issue of advising the suspect of his rights. Do it quickly, do it briefly, and do not repeat it, "I'm sure you want to know what this is all about and I will explain it to you, but first I have to take care of this advisement form. You've seen this on TV; you know I have to do this first." Read the advisement form to him, mark down his responses, and get him to sign it, then place the form out of sight in a drawer. An example of a Miranda form if given on page 18.

The importance of giving the warning promptly without prior questions is illustrated by the experience of Denver homicide Detective John D. Wyckoff. He was investigating the brutal sexual assault and murder of an 11-year-old girl at a country club swimming pool. Her body was found in a storage area accessible to only a few employees. One of them was James Lowe. He was brought to the homicide bureau and Detective Wyckoff's first question was, "Well, James, do you know why you are here?" The reply was, "I figured you would be out to talk to me."

Detective Wyckoff completed the advisement form and subsequently obtained a detailed confession of the sexual assault and fatal beating. Incriminating evidence was obtained on a search warrant based on the confession. During the trial the confession was suppressed because, in the opinion of the trial judge, when Detective Wyckoff asked "Do you know why you are here?" he was trying to elicit an incriminating response before giving the Miranda warning.

When reading the suspect his rights show that you already know his first, middle and last name as well as his date of birth. "Your name is John Henry Jones and your date of birth is November 5, 1971." This tells him that you are well prepared and he wonders what else you know about him.

When a citizen walks up to a police officer and blurts out a confession to a crime, there is no immediate need to interrupt him and advise him of his Miranda rights. However, you should advise him before asking him any questions. A bomb squad detective goes to an abortion clinic that had been bombed and asks a group of

ADVISEMENT FORM

Name_____ Birthdate_____

Date _____ Time_____

Location_____

You have a right to remain silent.

Anything you say can be used as evidence against you in court.

You have a right to talk to a lawyer before questioning and have him present during questioning.

If you cannot afford a lawyer, one will be appointed for you before questioning, if you wish.

Do you understand each of these rights I have read to you?

Answer _____

Signature of the Person Advised _____

Knowing my rights and knowing what I am doing, I now wish to voluntarily talk to you.

Signature of the Person Advised _____

Witnessed by _____

Signature of the Advising Officer _____

citizens at the scene, "Did anybody see what happened?" and a man replies: "I was pissed off at the abortion clinic, I told them to quit doing this, they didn't listen. I put the bomb there to get my point across, to get them to listen to me."

Wait until he has finished speaking, then take him aside and give him the Miranda warnings. After he has signed the waiver, tell him "I am going to take you to my office and I'm going to talk to you about this incident." Avoid statements like "I'm going to interrogate you" or "I'm going to question you."

Miranda warnings are not needed when life is at stake. For example when someone, especially a child, has been kidnapped and the police believe that the victim's life is in danger, the police can question the suspect without warning him that anything he says can be used in evidence against him and without offering him the services of an attorney. When the kidnappers have threatened to kill the victim if the ransom is not paid, there is clearly a threat to life. If a newborn baby has been kidnapped from a hospital, one can assume that there is a risk to the baby's life.

BEGIN WITH A POSITIVE STATEMENT

Open with a positive statement: "We're investigating an armed robbery and we think you can help us" or perhaps with an even stronger statement, such as "We're investigating the sexual assaults that you're involved in." A large case folder on the desk suggests that the investigation has revealed much information, yet the folder may contain records on another case.

PRELIMINARY SKIRMISHING

*Skirmish. An irregular engagement between two small
bodies of troops, especially detached or outlying portions
of opposing armies; a petty fight or encounter.*
                    Shorter Oxford English Dictionary

The opening statement is like a declaration of war. The suspect
has committed a crime, and the detective wants to know about it.
Sides have been drawn and there is a period of skirmishing before
the real battle begins. Each contestant assesses the other's
strengths and weaknesses. There may be quick capitulation with
confession, or at least partial confession, because it is difficult to
tell the whole truth at once. More often both sides settle down to
a long drawn out encounter. During this stage the detective assesses
the suspect's personality and tries to form a bond with the suspect.
The initial approach is usually low key.

In the hustle and bustle of the modern world, business is often
conducted in uncivilized haste. In former times such behavior was
considered ill-bred, and a gentleman would always pass the time
of day and inquire about another's health or well-being before mentioning vulgar commercial transactions. The interrogator would do
well to indulge in civilized pleasantries with the suspect before
questioning him about his felonious activities. "What are you doing
these days?" — "Oh I'm working for a burglar alarm company."
"What is your brother doing?" — "Ten to fifteen." You can see how
useful these questions can be. They make the suspect feel that you
are interested in him and not just in his crimes.

In this introductory phase of the questioning, the detective attempts to establish a friendly relationship and to win the confidence
and trust of the suspect. If the man has an Irish name, comment
on that. Irishmen are inordinately proud of their heritage. If a
suspect has an unusual name, inquire about it. David had to interview Banner Molinar, a Hispanic suspect in the shotgun slaying of
a McDonald's restaurant employee during an armed robbery. Banner is an unusual first name for a Spanish American, so his family

was questioned about this. It was the name of his uncle who was killed in 1943 in World War II. He was born ten years later on the anniversary of his uncle's death. After Banner was arrested following his advisement he was told, "You're not a bad guy, you come from a decent family. Your uncle was killed in World War II, you were named after him." This opening helped establish a good relationship and probably contributed to his confession.

Ask the suspect where he lives; has he always lived in that part of town; where did he grow up? It is surprising how often these questions can provide useful information or lead to further informal discussion that brings both parties together. It is helpful for the interrogator to find something that he shares with the suspect, whether is is an interest in pickup trucks, football, service in the Marine Corps or even an awareness of some slang expression. An uncooperative black suspect was asked by a detective who had worked in the South, "Were you ever caught toting sugar?" (meaning moonshine). After this question, the suspect became quite friendly.

Every person has something he is proud of, whether it is his skill at basketball, his intellect, his sense of honor, loyalty to companions, muscular development, physical appearance, cooking skills or independence. Attention should be directed to his source of pride. An uncooperative soldier suspected of strangling his girlfriend responded quickly after his biceps were felt and favorably appraised. A poorly educated but intelligent murderer confessed after his interest in books and wide range of knowledge were remarked upon. Keep in mind: The small man may lift weights and work out to compensate for his small stature; the man who uses words a college graduate might not understand may be compensating for dropping out of school in the fourth grade. You won't find these things out unless you check the first man's biceps and ask the second man about his school record.

It is surprising how often a kind approach leads to an admission of the crime, even in hardened offenders. Some detectives are perhaps overly friendly, showing excessive concern for the suspect's welfare. Such an approach is likely to arouse the same suspicion that a car buyer has for a sugary used-car salesman. It is sufficient to offer a soft drink or a cup of coffee, but don't overdo it.

It is often a good idea to offer the suspect a cigarette. This offer creates goodwill, but smoking relieves anxiety, and John prefers to ask the suspect if he would mind not smoking until the interview is over. I explain that I am allergic to cigarette smoke. There is, however, the risk that you will cause offense.

If you sense that a request not to smoke is going to cause a problem, reconsider your decision. John was asked to examine a man who had stabbed to death a municipal bus driver who refused to hand over his bus. This man was clearly schizophrenic and very dangerous. After the first interview John always brought him a pack of cigarettes at each interview. The first concern was to relieve his anxiety so that an examination could be completed without injury. Shortly after John's last visit he attacked a deputy sheriff who had to be hospitalized.

Not all policemen adopt a casual, friendly approach. Sergeant Bill Parker of the Dallas Police Department has a different style, "Nobody wants to do business with a shoe salesman, so I try to build up my own prestige (in the suspect's eyes). I don't go fetch him myself, I have him brought to me. I don't bring a prisoner coffee or take him to the bathroom. I want him to end up thinking that he is dealing with a pretty powerful person. What I'm communicating to him is that I have power over him and that I don't even have to dirty my hands to exert it."

Regardless of one's preferred style of interviewing, a firm, distant attitude may be the best approach, especially when the suspect shows a negative response to a more intimate approach. A reserved, senior business executive might resent the use of his first name. It is sometimes better to move slowly, to test the water, before plunging in. In general, one shows interest, courtesy and respect. The time has come to ask about the crime.

THE SUSPECT'S ACCOUNT OF THE CRIME

"Where shall I begin, please your Majesty?" asked the
White Rabbit. "Begin at the beginning," the King said
gravely, "and go on till you come to the end: then stop."
Lewis Carrol, *Alice's Adventures in Wonderland*

When a suspect is questioned about a crime, he should be allowed to tell his story without interruption. If he mentions that he drove to the area of the crime in his girlfriend's car, do not interrupt him with questions on the make, model, color and year of the car. Such questions interrupt the flow of conversation and can always be asked later. They also tend to place him on guard and reduce the interview to a series of direct questions and answers. A.J. Liebling expresses this viewpoint well:

"I had a distaste for asking direct questions, a practice I considered ill-bred. This handicapped me not as much as you might think. Direct questions tighten a man up, and even if he answers, he will not tell you anything you have not asked him. What you want is to get him to tell his story. After he has, you can ask clarifying questions such as, 'How did you come to have the axe in your hand?'"

If the suspect talks at very great length on events before the crime, or if he goes into a great deal of irrelevant detail, it may become necessary to move him along. In general, however, it is especially important at this stage to keep in mind the admonition "Don't be talking when you should be listening." It may be necessary to reveal some of your evidence of his involvement in the crime to get him started, but like a good poker player you should not reveal all the cards you hold. Don't provide information only the suspect would know.

Do not make any false statements. Do not tell him his fingerprints were found at the scene if they were not found at the scene. Do not tell him he was identified by an eyewitness if he was not identified by an eyewitness. If he catches you in a false statement, he will no longer trust you, he will assume that you do not have sufficient evidence to prove his guilt, and his self-confidence will go up.

For example, he may know that you don't have his fingerprints because he was wearing gloves.

If the suspect makes a statement that you know to be untrue, do not immediately confront him. If he wishes to tell tall tales, allow him to do so. If he wants to dig a ditch for himself, let him do so. Let him bury himself in a host of contradictions, inconsistencies, improbable explanations and false statements. These will make him vulnerable to sudden, massive confrontation and will also weaken his position in court. When he has finished explaining his behavior at the time of the crime, direct questioning on many issues becomes necessary.

Make sure that every aspect of the crime has been covered. Do not restrict yourself to the victim's account of what has happened, as the victim may have withheld information. For example, a rape victim, through embarrassment and humiliation, may not mention that the suspect pushed the barrel of his revolver in her vagina. If you are not familiar with the crime under investigation, check the relevant chapter in this book to make sure that you have not overlooked a frequent feature of the crime. Rare or relatively rare features should also be the subject of inquiry, for example the burglar's visiting card (his feces at the scene). Also keep in mind the criminal profiles of various offenders such as child molesters, rapists, arsonists and organized and disorganized murderers.

MAKING IT EASIER FOR THE SUSPECT TO CONFESS

When the suspect does not give a full account of his participation in the crime or claims innocence, help him to speak more frankly. Ask him about any stresses that were affecting him at the time of the crime, — family problems, spouse or lover threatening to leave, separation, divorce, pregnant wife, sick child, sickness or death in the family, accident, civil lawsuit, recent arrest, financial difficulties, trouble at work, whatever. Ask him whether he has any emotional problems, has he seen a psychiatrist or thought of seeing one. You can understand how someone might do something he would not think of doing, if he was not under the influence of alcohol or drugs (if that was the case).

Make no threats, make no promises. For example, do not promise release on bond, reduction of charges, dropping charges, a shorter sentence or probation. One can tell the suspect that if he cooperates in the investigation, the district attorney will be informed of this.

In a homicide, had the victim threatened him, did he really intend to shoot him, had he planned it out in advance, or was it something that just happened? Above all do not at this stage emphasize or even refer to the seriousness of the offense. If anything, downplay the seriousness of the offense: "This type of thing happens all the time," "I understand how this could have happened," "It's not all that unusual."

When clearly the victim has provoked the crime, reference to this may facilitate admission of the offense. Curiously some suspects downplay provocation by the victim. This is particularly likely in the murder of a brutal father by a battered child. Husbands or wives who feel guilty for having killed their spouse may not reveal the full extent of possible extenuating factors. After these have been explored they may be able to admit their guilt.

Many offenders are reluctant to inform on their partners in crime. One method of easing this burden is to tell the suspect, "I'm going to go out of the room. When I come back, if I find a name on this piece of paper, no one can ever say you told me." Another approach is to say "Was Frank the other guy?" If the suspect becomes ill at ease, which suggests that Frank was in fact his partner, but he does not want to be labeled a snitch, tell him, "I know you don't want to be a snitch, but if you were me, would you put Frank's picture in the mug shot book and show it to the victims? Nobody will ever know how it got there." If he replies, "It might not be a bad idea," you have the information you need.

INTERVIEWING TECHNIQUES

You know my methods, Watson.

Conan Doyle,
The Memoirs of
Sherlock Holmes

There are some basic techniques of interviewing that have to be kept in mind at all times. Failure to obtain a confession from a suspect or significant information from a witness may be the result of failure to observe one or more of the following rules.

Ask One Question At A Time

Whenever you ask several questions in the same sentence, the chances are that you will not notice the failure of the suspect to answer one or more of these questions. The suspect will take care to avoid answering the question that he finds most troublesome. Indeed, he will try to distract the detective's attention from his failure to answer this question by talking at length on other subjects.

A public defender in a robbery-rape-homicide trial claimed that the defendant's confession during a taperecorded interrogation was inadmissible because his client was under the influence of drugs. John testified to the effect that the confession was admissible, but the detective's last question did cause some problems. The question was, "Do you know what you're saying; do you feel like you're under the influence of anything; or are you aware of what's going on and what you're saying?"

There were four questions and the suspect answered only one of them. He replied, "I'm aware of what I'm saying," and the detective said, "This will end the tape." The suspect never answered the question of whether he was under the influence of anything.

Make Sure Your Question Has Been Answered

A suspect may start to answer the detective's question and then shift to some topic likely to arouse the detective's interest. The change of topic may not be sudden and obvious, rather the suspect's answer seems to lead naturally into another but perhaps related matter. The unsolved murder of a police officer or the unsolved brutal rape-murder of a six-year-old child immediately captures the attention of the interrogator, especially when the suspect hints that he knows the identity of the slayer or that he has heard talk on the street that might help solve the crime. After further discussion the detective resumes his inquiry but forgets that the suspect did not answer the last question about his crime.

John always writes down questions and answers, especially key questions. This makes it much easier to make sure that all key questions have in fact been answered.

Questions Should Be Clear Cut and Not Ambiguous

It is better to ask "May I see your ID" than to ask "Do you have any ID?" Sure he has some ID but he neglects to say that it is someone else's ID, after all he wasn't asked for his ID.

Even such an experienced investigator as Inspector Clousseau made this elementary mistake. He was about to pat a dog in the lobby of a hotel, he hesitated and asked the hotel manager, "Does your dog bite?" "No," replied the manager, but when the inspector patted the dog he was promptly bitten on the hand. He complained to the manager, "I asked you if your dog bites," and the manager replied "That's not my dog."

Ask Specific and General Questions

If the victim reports that $450 was stolen from the safe, the suspect should be asked if he took $450 from the safe. There is always the possibility that there was more or less money in the safe, so that the suspect can look you straight in the eye and truthfully deny taking the money, after all he took $450 and some loose change. It is necessary to ask the additional question, "Did you take any money from the safe?" He will probably deny the theft, but this time he may betray his untruthfulness by looking away or through other nonverbal behavior.

Curiously, suspects will sometimes tell the truth when questioned either accurately or in general terms. For example, a man charged in federal court with kidnapping denied having a red handled ice pick in his van. Yet when asked if he had any ice pick in his van, he acknowledged that he had an ice pick with a rust colored handle in his van. A surprising number of criminals will give helpful answers providing they are asked the right questions. The broad question, "What did you do after leaving San Francisco?" — "I took a United Airlines flight to Denver," should be followed by the very narrow question, "Was it a nonstop flight?" — "No, I spent three days in Las Vegas." The suspect's activities during these three days may be revealing, but they might have escaped notice in the absence of the important second question.

Antisocial personalities interpret questions in very concrete ways to suit their own convenience. For example, an antisocial personality in a city jail may deny that he has ever been in jail. That is, he interprets a question on this point as meaning has he ever been in this jail before, and he has not been in that particular jail before. An inquiry about residence in a penitentiary may reveal that he has been in San Quentin. A further question about any other penitentiaries elicits a negative response, since he thinks the detective still has in mind state penitentiaries; so he sees no point in mentioning a long stay in Leavenworth, which is a federal penitentiary. Yet he will quickly mention Leavenworth if asked about federal penitentiaries.

Choose Your Words Carefully

Avoid harsh words such as murder, rape and stabbing. It is better to ask "Did you make love to her?" than to ask "Did you rape her?" "Was he cut?" suggests that the knife just happened to fly through the air and land in the other person's chest, almost as if the suspect had nothing to do with the victim's death. It all sounds so much more innocuous than "Did you stab him?" "Were you driving by that rich attorney's house with the Mercedes parked in the driveway?" shows that the detective can understand how a burglar with a heroin habit can be tempted in these circumstances. He may even have the mistaken impression that the detective shares his dislike of attorneys. Every effort should be made to make confession as painless as possible.

Catch The Suspect By Surprise

The suspect may be disconcerted by the unexpected attitude and manner of the interrogator. There is an adage, "Treat a duchess like a whore, and a whore like a duchess." Unexpected kindness will often catch an offender off guard. A woman charged with murder did not answer any questions, but after she was given some picture postcards to send to her children she cried and began talking about her crime. She said later that she had expected an angry response to her initial failure to answer.

The occasional question that has no relation to the crime puzzles the suspect, and his answer may, if only by chance, contribute to a better understanding of his personality. Routinely the psychiatric author asks, "What kind of car do you drive?" and the answers are sometimes of psychological interest. A young woman who had burned her parents to death, when asked this question some years after the incident, said she drove a red Pontiac Firebird.

A detective should not hesitate to ask questions based on his hunches. If his intuitive guess proves correct, the suspect will often be caught by surprise and will assume either that the detective is an insightful person or that he has important sources of information. John once asked a suspect if he had ever been a police officer, and he replied that he had been a police cadet for several months. Later, wondering why he had asked that question, John remembered that the suspect had told him that he "worked out" regularly lifting weights, an activity favored by many police officers.

Vary The Approach

A technique that has long been used by detectives is for one officer, usually an older detective, to adopt a brusque, unsympathetic manner, while his younger colleague, who plays a less active role in the questioning, is friendly and understanding in his manner.

When the stern detective leaves the interviewing room, the younger detective, using a low-key approach, is often successful in obtaining a confession. The "hot-cold" approach can be used by a single interrogator, who is cold and remote at one interviewing session, then warm and kind at the next session.

Rephrase Questions

Important questions should be asked again in different ways. Rephrasing a question gives the suspect the opportunity to give an honest answer without losing face. It may be necessary to rephrase the question because the suspect did not understand it. "Did you have sexual intercourse with this woman?" "No" — "Do you know what you were arrested for?" — "Yes." "What for?" — "For fucking her." "That's what I have been asking you." The offender did not know the meaning of the term sexual intercourse.

A man who confessed ten rapes repeatedly denied wearing gloves during his offenses. Finally one of the detectives asked him if he was wearing anything on his hands, and he revealed that he had socks on his hands.

Try Indirect Questions

During an interrogation a suspect was asked "Where's Bob living these days?" He replied "You mean Bob O'Hayre?" — "Yes." "Well I don't know where he's living." But he had answered the real question, which had not been asked directly, "Who is Bob?" During one of his armed robberies he had called his partner Bob.

Avoid Questions That Can Be Answered Yes Or No

Sometimes one should avoid questions that can be answered yes or no. Thus instead of asking "Was John there?" ask "Who was there?" followed by "Anyone else?" "Nobody? Are you sure?"

Cautiously Use Leading Questions

Leading questions are usually asked when the detective already knows the answers, but there is a danger in asking leading questions. You may reveal information about the crime to all the suspects, and eventually information, which should be known only by the offender and the detectives, becomes public knowledge. It becomes possible for people to make false confessions, which can become an embarrassment.

When a confession is obtained after prolonged questioning, without the use of leading questions, the decision may be made to get the suspect to make a written statement or to repeat the confession on videotape. In order to do this quickly the suspect may be asked a series of leading questions. In court he claims that the detective put words in his mouth and he answered yes to all the questions because of threats or promises. Thus it is very important to avoid such use of leading questions. Instead of asking "Did you shoot him three times?" ask "How many times did you shoot him?" Instead of asking "Did you throw the gun in the creek?" ask "What did you do with the gun?"

Excuse the Crime

Suspects find it easier to confess when they can offer some face-saving reason for committing the crime. Sometimes there are extenuating circumstances. For example, one-quarter to one-third of criminal homicides are victim-precipitated because the victim is the first to resort to physical violence. In these homicides the victim is the first to show and to use a deadly weapon or to strike a blow in an altercation. In these cases, the victim is more likely than the offender to have a prior criminal record.

If the interrogator has reason to suspect, or if he does not know whether a crime is victim-precipitated, it is permissible for him to raise this possibility in questioning the suspect. He should not, however, raise this issue if he knows that the crime was clearly not victim-precipitated. There should always be a good-faith approach without dishonesty in criminal interrogation.

The detective can point out that evidence of planning can lead to a conviction of first-degree murder; that a fight in a bar where there was no prior plan to murder can lead to conviction on a charge of second-degree murder; that when death occurs without intent to kill, as for example the death of a man who falls in a fight and strikes his head on the curb, there may be a verdict of manslaughter; and that a killing in self-defense may lead to a finding of justifiable homicide. He may also point out that the account of the tragedy, provided to the investigating detective is more likely to be believed than a revised explanation provided several months later at the trial.

If a homicide suspect claims that he shot the victim accidentally, during a fight for possession of a revolver, his account of the event, even if false, may be of vital importance. Without this admission it might not be possible to prove in court that he was at the crime scene and that he fired the revolver. The autopsy findings can be used to prove that the gunshot wounds were not consistent with his account of firing the weapon during a struggle for possession of it.

The detective can ask a bank employee, suspected of embezzling thousands of dollars, "Did you do this to pay for your child's hospital bills, or did you do it for your lover?" If it was a sexual offense, did the victim lead him on, was she promiscuous, did he think she was older than 14? A father, suspected of incest, can be told that his daughter looks older than her age, if this is true.

Other excuses, which do not relieve the suspect of criminal responsibility may also be proffered, as for example: "Do you think the use of drugs had anything to do with this?" "You said you were really drunk that day, do you think that had something to do with this?" "If you were not upset over your wife saying she was going to divorce you, do you think you would have been involved in this?"

Any hint or statement that an accomplice in an armed robbery has accused the suspect of shooting the victim, may lead to an admission of participating in the robbery but a denial of use of a weapon. Any falling out among partners in crime is to the advantage of the police, and detectives can foster such disputes.

Confront the Suspect

The decision may be made to confront the suspect with numerous indications of his guilt in the initial interview. This may be successful with the first offender who feels overwhelmed by the shock of his arrest and by his feelings of guilt. The career criminal or the more confident first-offender is not likely to collapse so easily, and it is better to delay confrontation. The clever antisocial personality, when confronted, is often quick to think of explanations for apparent inconsistencies in his statement.

If, however, he is suddenly faced with many inconsistencies in quick succession, one after another, he becomes mentally fatigued and he may throw in the towel, admitting his guilt. If he does not confess, he may make statements that point to his guilt. For example, one suspect, toward the end of a long interrogation, on being told that a witness had identified him replied, "It was too dark in that place and the broad was too scared." It may be helpful to point out body language, such as covering the eyes or not looking at the detective when talking about the crime or some aspect of it.

Persist

There is a general rule that you should continue questioning for fifteen minutes after you have decided to stop. One should not become discouraged as interrogation is sometimes an endurance contest. There are times, however, when one should not persist. For example, when a suspect is confessing to a series of armed robberies but inexplicably denies involvement in his third robbery. It may be better to move on to the next robbery as he may not only resist persistent questioning on his third robbery, but decide not to say anything further. So long as he is confessing, keep moving with him. When he has finished you can come back to the crimes he has denied committing.

CONTROL OF THE INTERROGATION

At all times the interrogator should be in control. This does not mean that he should be domineering, although he may be forceful when indicated. Indeed he may be quite passive at times when it suits his purpose. Yet even when passive he remains in control of the interview. Self-control is important. John had to interview an armed robber who went from room to room killing occupants of a home. He had previously tied them up. His account of the triple slaying was upsetting, and John's face betrayed his distress. The murderer rebuked him saying: "You shouldn't let yourself be emotionally involved. You should be cool, detached and clinical. A good psychiatrist should cultivate that ability."

The detective should try to conceal any negative feelings he may have toward the suspect. If you become angry and insulting, the suspect may conclude that you are frustrated because you do not have enough evidence to press charges against him, and this strengthens his resistance to interrogation. If the detective has arrested a homicide suspect after a chase or a shootout, his adrenalin will be flowing and he may have strong negative feelings toward his prisoner. The detective should compose himself, perhaps walking around the block, before starting the interview.

David has never seen a successful outcome when an interrogation has been conducted by a detective who has obvious feelings of anger toward the suspect. In contrast, John considers that occasionally it may be rewarding to express negative feelings toward the suspect, as in the following example:

A 21-year-old man charged with murder boasted of previous acts of violence. He threatened to kill John if he was pushed too far. When another prisoner threatened to attack John, the suspect shouted encouraging comments from his cell, placing John in greater danger. Later, John explained to him that he was capable of better behavior. The next day he apologized, saying "I feel much better because you got mad at me yesterday and put me in my place. I respect you now, you told me to fuck myself yesterday, only you used nice words." He became more cooperative and provided additional information about himself and the murder.

The suspect may attempt to control the interview by talking at length but not to the point. He may attempt to intimidate you by threats of violence to you or your family, or by claims of political influence. One should not be ruffled by such efforts to impede the investigation.

Female suspects may try to control the interrogation by crying or through seductive behavior. If the suspect does not have a tissue to wipe away her tears, one can be provided. It may be helpful to express a word of sympathy, but the questioning should continue. You will ask yourself whether the suspect is expressing genuine emotion, or is she testing you to see whether she can manipulate you? A businesslike attitude reduces the risk of seductive behavior. If necessary, the presence of a female detective will take care of the problem.

THE SUSPECT'S COMMENTS

The Gratuitous Statement

Former FBI Agent R.E. Vorpagel warns to watch out for the gratuitous statement and quotes the case of the homicide suspect who volunteered, "I hitchhiked to Yosemite Park. I didn't come by car." Why did he add that he didn't come by car? A search of the park revealed the car that he had borrowed to drive to the park. The victim's bloody clothing was in the trunk.

Inconsistent Statements

Not all inconsistent statements indicate guilt. It is better to delay confrontation, as this may alert the suspect and hinder your inquiry.

Lies

In Paul Ekman's *Telling Lies: Clues to Deceit in the Market Place, Politics and Marriage* he says there are two primary ways to lie: to conceal and to falsify. "In concealing, the liar withholds some information without actually saying anything untrue. In falsifying, an additional step is taken. Not only does the liar withhold true information, but he presents false information as if it were true. Often it is necessary to combine concealing and falsifying to pull off the deceit, but sometimes a liar can get away with just concealment . . . When there is a choice about how to lie, liars usually prefer concealing to falsifying. There are many advantages. For one thing, concealing usually is easier than falsifying. Nothing has to be made up . . . Concealment lies are also much easier to cover afterward if discovered. The liar does not go as far out on a limb. There are many available excuses—ignorance, the intent to reveal it later, memory failure and so on."

The interrogator should make a note of both lies through falsification and of lies through concealment. In the early stages of the investigation, the interrogator may not always be aware that the suspect has lied to him. Hence the importance of keeping careful records of interviews, so that later one can show to the court or to the suspect that he concealed or falsified information.

CLUES TO DECEPTION

Brief Answers

The suspect who gives only brief answers is almost certainly lying through concealment of information.

Excessively Detailed Answers

Suspects who go into very great detail in describing events not directly connected to the crime, usually events preceding or following the crime, are often the perpetrators.

Repeating the Question

By repeating the question put to him, "What do you mean by asking me. . ." "Did I ever use cocaine?" or "Did I meet Joe at the corner of Colfax and Race?" the suspect gains time to think of an answer.

Rephrasing the Question

"So you want to know if I ever used cocaine?" Once again the suspect wants time to think of an answer. The person who has never used cocaine gives an immediate negative response.

Hesitation in Answering

Hesitation in answering important questions, which should not require a moment's consideration, is a good indication of deception. Pauses during an answer with many "um's" and "ah's" strengthen suspicion.

Memory Problems

"I don't remember" and "I can't recall" may be reasonable answers to questions about events on an unremarkable day three months previously, but "I can't recall torturing anyone" seems a little strange. Be very suspicious of "Not that I can remember" responses regarding events that are unlikely to pass from one's memory. Murders, rapes, robberies, assaults and burglaries are not quickly forgotten. Do not lightly accept claims of loss of memory due to the use of alcohol or drugs.

Qualified Answers

Guilty suspects will often qualify their answers. "That is correct, but . . ." or "Yes, to the best of my recollection." "It could be, maybe I'm not sure." "It might be." "As far as I know I wasn't there."

References to Honesty

Regard with the gravest suspicion such statements as: "I swear to God," "I swear by my mother," "To tell you the truth," "Honestly," "Truthfully," "Frankly," "They can send me to jail for the rest of my life, but I didn't do it" and "Do you think I'm a liar?" Such comments at the very outset of a criminal interrogation strongly suggest deception.

References to Religion

"I'll swear on a stack of Bibles," "May the Lord bless you," "May God strike me dead if I'm not telling you the truth," "I didn't rape her, as God is my witness," "I swear to God," "Ask my minister (pastor or priest)" and "I'm a deacon at my church" all arouse immediate suspicion because of the inappropriate context in which these comments are made.

Softening Terms of Violence and Theft

The innocent suspect uses blunt terms in denying guilt, the guilty suspect uses softer terms as if to diminish the significance of his felonious acts. Thus, the innocent suspect will say, "I didn't murder him" and "I didn't multilate his body." Whereas the guilty suspect will say "I didn't hurt him" and "I didn't cut him." "I didn't steal the money" becomes "I didn't take the money," and "I didn't rape her" becomes "I didn't touch her."

Speaking in the Third Person

A sudden shift by the suspect from talking in the first person to talking in the third person is a bad sign; it is as though the suspect wants to distance himself from the interrogation and from the crime. "It is possible that he could have done that."

Over-Politeness or Irritability

Beware of the obsequious, mealy-mouthed suspect who admires your shiny polyester suit, and comments on the education needed to become a detective. "Do you mind if I say something, Sir?" "I really admire the work you're doing on this case." Beware also of the irritable, hypercritical suspect who has nothing good to say about the police department. "I've already talked to one detective, do I have to go over this again?"

Short-Lived Anger

The innocent as well as the guilty suspect can show great anger when questioned about a murder, armed robbery, sexual assault or lesser crime. The innocent suspect will continue to express outrage, but the guilty suspect's anger is often curiously short-lived.

BODY LANGUAGE

There are often voice and words in a silent look.

Ovid

Actions sometimes speak louder than words. The armed robber who jacks a shell in his shotgun conveys a deadly message. A change in facial expression "if looks could kill," can convey greater menace than the spoken word. In these two examples the criminal uses body language to reveal his intentions or thoughts, but body language can also be used to conceal thoughts and feelings.

Thus a suspect's angry response to the interrogator's line of questioning can be concealed behind a smile. There are limits to such deception because the false smile lacks spontaneity and the characteristic wrinkling of the skin at the corners of the eyes. There is a Cantonese proverb that warns, "Watch out for the man whose stomach doesn't move when he laughs."

Involuntary bodily reactions are of the greatest importance in criminal interrogation. In *Criminal Psychology*, Hans Gross points out that simple and significant gestures often contradict false statements. A suspect says, "She went down," but he points up. Here the speech was false and the gesture true. Gross notes that the speaker had to turn all his attention on what he wanted to say so that the unwatched co-consciousness moved his hand.

Gross cites other examples: "A remarkable case of this kind was that of a suspect of child murder. The girl told that she had given birth to the child all alone, had washed it, and then laid it on the bed beside herself. She had also observed how a corner of the coverlet had fallen on the child's face, and thought it might interfere with the child's breathing; but at this point she swooned, was unable to help the child and it was choked. While sobbing and weeping as she was telling the story, she spread the fingers of her left hand and pressed it on her thigh, as perhaps she might have done, if she had first put something soft, the corner of a coverlet possibly, over the child's nose and mouth, and then pressed on it. This action was so clearly significant that it inevitably led to the question whether she hadn't choked the child in that way. She assented, sobbing.

"Similar is another case in which a man assured us that he lived very peaceably with his neighbor and at the same time clenched his fist. The latter meant ill will toward the neighbor while the words did not."

The interrogator should watch for any nonverbal communication that may show the need for further inquiry. Slightly hesitant speech for the first time, a change in the tone of voice or rate of speech, twisting of a lock of hair, a flush rising from the base of the neck or a sudden downward look may all suggest that the whole truth is not being told. A sudden interest in something in the interviewing room may point to deception as in the following example:

A middle-aged, chronic alcoholic man, who pleaded not guilty by reason of insanity to a charge of murder, was friendly and cooperative on psychiatric examination by John. He spoke freely and when questioned directly on any subject he replied without hesitation. It was noted that he appeared somewhat ill at ease when describing his school record. The subject was therefore raised again at a later interview and once more he appeared somewhat discomforted. His answers were not as spontaneous as previously. He turned half away and appeared to be interested in the contents of a glass medicine cabinet. In view of his change in demeanor, it was assumed he was withholding information.

He denied this, but became more obviously distressed. Then suddenly, with considerable release of feeling, he revealed that at the age of 12 he had seen his father shot and killed by a revenue officer. He had rushed to grab his father's loaded shotgun, went outside and killed the revenue officer. His placement in a reform school had interfered with his schooling. On his release from prison he went to another state, married and settled down.

This man had been successful in keeping this information a secret from his wife for their 30 years of married life. The earlier murder conviction was not on his police records, but was confirmed by correspondence with the reform school.

CLUES TO DECEPTION

Ekman wisely warns that, "A lie catcher should never rely upon one clue to deceit; there must be many." Nevertheless, one clue is sometimes sufficient. Beware of the suspect who holds his hand over his mouth with his thumb on his cheek. It is almost as if he is ashamed of his lies and is trying to hide their source. Touching the nose is a variant of this gesture. Perhaps the suspect intended to cover his mouth, thought better of it and touched or rubbed the end of his nose instead.

Similarly the suspect who holds a hand over his eyes may be ashamed of himself. He does not want to see the interrogator or be seen by him. He may rub his eyes or avoid eye contact. The suspect who is aware of the significance of diminished eye contact may go out of his way to look the interrogator in the eye. Such prolonged eye contact suggests deception. The shifty-eyed person may make a point of looking you in the eye after he has told a lie.

The suspect who becomes uncomfortable while looking you in the eye may disguise an eye-break by looking at his fingers or at his wedding ring. The "con man" maintains good eye contact. One of the things that attracted Patricia Gardner to Giovanni Vigliotto, the man who may have married 100 women, was "that honest trait" of looking directly into her eyes, she testified at his trial for bigamy.

Link and Foster in *The Kinesic Interview Technique* emphasize the significance of "three whites of the eyes." The eye in the normal state, unless a person is looking sharply upward, has white only on the sides of the iris. They point out that many people under heavy stress will show white under the iris as well, even when they are looking straight ahead. The presence of three whites of the eyes in only one of a group of suspects or witnesses present at the scene of a crime, suggests the one person who should be selected for questioning in depth. The appearance for the first time of three whites of the eye during an interrogation, suggests that the detective has touched on an area that is troubling to the subject.

The suspect who puts his hand over his ear or around the lower part of his ear may be saying to himself "I don't want to hear what you're saying, nor what I'm telling you." He may rub his ear or clean his ear with his little finger. Another gesture that may occur when a person is telling a lie is pulling on a shirt collar as if it is too tight or to increase the circulation of air beneath the shirt.

There are many nervous gestures to relieve tension by taking the person's mind off the subject under discussion, such as: thread pulling, lint picking, smoothing a dress, stroking hair, cleaning glasses, inspecting or biting fingernails, sighing, yawning, tapping a foot or drumming fingertips on a desk. Knuckle cracking tends to distract the interrogator.

Other Body Signals

The suspect who sits upright, tense, with his arms crossed, and possibly with his feet crossed also, is trying to block you out. His lips are tightly pressed together. He does not want to talk to you. Suspects never confess with their arms or legs crossed, or their ankles locked. If he leans away from you, he is telling you that he would prefer to be elsewhere. He might even sit poised on the edge of his chair, with one foot out and one bent at the knee, like a runner, waiting for the starting signal.

If you gain his cooperation, his posture may become relaxed, with his hands on his knees or by his side. If his head droops forward and his body slumps down in his chair with his hands between his legs, this may be an indication that he is about to confess. Suddenly all the air has gone out of him. If, however, he takes a deep breath and sits up, he is letting you know that some of his confidence has returned. You will have to keep talking to him. You have almost succeeded. If a male suspect cries, you have reached a critical stage of the interview—push it.

Coughing, slowly putting out a cigarette, taking off and cleaning glasses, all give suspects time to think of an answer. The person who scratches the back of his head is either uncertain of his answer or he is lying.

The suspect who leans forward is reacting favorably. This may be the time to invade his body space and to ask vital questions regarding his guilt. If he backs away from you, delay confrontation. The man who shrugs his shoulders is saying, "I don't know," "I'm helpless" or "What does it matter?" Ekman found that some women shrug with just one hand, rotating it a bit, or they rotate both hands, while the hands stayed in the lap.

It has been suggested that the man who looks up when he is asked a question may be trying to visualize the event under discussion. He should be asked "Can you see what I am talking about?" The man who looks to one side is trying to recall what was said. He should be asked "Can you hear what I'm saying?" The man who looks down is feeling or touching oriented. He should be asked "Can you feel what I'm getting at?"

JUVENILE SUSPECTS

Younger juvenile suspects are likely to talk to detectives, either because this is their first encounter with the police, or because they know that nothing will happen to them. Unless it is a serious offense the young juvenile offender is usually given a lecture and released. You can often tell at a glance whether a suspect is fearful, cocky, sullen, streetwise, eager to please or remorseful. His developmental age or emotional maturity is as important as his actual age. There are 14-year-old adults and 36-year-old children. Some children are more streetwise than their parents.

As with adult suspects, care should be taken not to bungle the initial meeting. It can be a good investment of time to help a youngster feel at ease. His fear of police, perhaps derived from hearing his father say "I'd better slow down, there's a cop there," may extend to the detective in plain clothes. The comments of experienced detectives are instructive:

"I can interrogate and the kid doesn't know he's being interrogated. I do anything I can to make them realize I'm human. I just sit down and talk. I like them to feel I'm just another person. 'That's a pretty blouse you have on.' I don't say I'm a detective, I tell them my name and that I've been assigned this matter. I advise them of their rights. Then I tell them this is the complaint, this is what you're supposed to have done, I'd like to discuss this matter with you. I don't talk over his head, I don't talk down to him. I treat him the way I would want someone to treat my kid. I treat the parents the way I would want to be treated.

"If he is a first-timer caught in a minor offense and ordered to report to the juvenile bureau the following day with his parents, I might take his belongings from him as if he is under arrest and have him sit in a holding cell. This has an impact on him. If he is 10 to 13 years old, I will tell him that I'm not here to lock him up, I will point out what he has done wrong, and what he should do to avoid coming back. If he has an inferiority complex and doesn't feel worthy of decent friends I'll call the school and arrange for counseling.

"I let them do the talking, you get further than if you do the talking. If they lie, I let them lie until they trap themselves. I don't use the word punish, but the harder the kid is the harder I am. I make it clear—you screwed up, you pay for it. I don't beat around the bush, I don't pull any punches."

In some states a juvenile cannot be questioned unless a parent or guardian is present. The juvenile is given the opportunity to talk to the parent alone before reaching a decision. You should not tell him, "If you don't want to talk you are free to leave." Usually the law only requires you to advise the juvenile of his rights in the presence of a parent or guardian and then leave them alone to discuss the matter. Some juveniles find it difficult to admit their misdeeds when they can see the face of their father or mother. For this reason it is a good idea to seat the parents in such a way that the juvenile does not see them.

Parents are often protective of a son or daughter and openly critical of the police. They have a natural inclination to believe in the innocence of their offspring and to be suspicious of police harassment. If, however, the detective's questions and the juvenile's answers begin to raise doubt in a parent's mind, there is gradually a change in attitude. Juveniles are quick to sense loss of parental support and this lessens their self-confidence. Sometimes parents take over the questioning from the detective and they are less likely to observe the restrictions placed on detectives by the courts.

TAKING NOTES

He listens to good purpose who takes note.

Dante, *Inferno*

The detective, by taking notes, may put an end to the interview. Even if the suspect raises no objection he may become much more careful in his choice of words. The detective with a good memory will prefer not to write anything down until he obtains a confession. Other detectives prefer to take notes after a "working relationship" has been established. The advantage of note-taking is that there is a reliable record, which can be reviewed later. One is not at the mercy of one's memory. Something that seems unimportant may later turn out to be significant. Apparently unimportant statements fade more quickly from memory.

Although most experts strongly advise against taking notes from the outset, there are times when you can do this. You begin by writing down neutral information such as the suspect's name, date of birth, address and so on. Many suspects seem to become accustomed to the constant note-taker. If, however, the detective only makes a few notes, this alerts the suspect to matters that seem important to the detective.

VIDEOTAPING

If the suspect in a serious crime is willing, a videotaped statement should be obtained. "Just so there will be no mistakes in what you want to tell us, let's videotape this." While a stenographer or tape recorder can provide a complete and accurate account of what is said in an interview, the videotape can do much more by showing the suspect's demeanor and appearance, mental and physical condition, attitude, injuries or absence of injuries, tone of voice, eye movements, gestures, body language and other nonverbal communication.

Large clear diagrams of the crime scene posted on a bulletin board hanging on the wall of the videotape interview room can be used by the suspect to clarify his account of the crime. He can use color crayons to show his position and movements at the crime scene, as well as the locations and movements of others. The weapon used to commit the crime, the proceeds of the crime and other evidence can be identified by the suspect and recorded on the videotape.

In an adjacent room other detectives can watch the interview on a television screen and they can provide suggestions to the interrogator when he leaves the videotape room to consult them. The videotape can be reviewed by investigators on the case who were not present at the interview, by prosecutors who have to make case filing decisions and present the case in court, by defense attorneys who must decide whether to plead their client guilty, by judges who make suppression of evidence decisions, by psychiatrists who evaluate the sanity of the suspect, and by jurors who determine the issue of guilt or innocence.

Claims of improper conduct by police, such as brutality, threats, intimidation, promises, or failure to advise the suspect of his constitutional rights can be judged by review of the videotape. To avoid difficulty in court, the interviewer should always introduce himself and all those present, state the time and date from the calendar and clock on the wall, tell the suspect that the session is being audio- and video-recorded, state the crime under investigation, the location and date, refer to prior Miranda advisement and repeat it on the tape.

You should not question the suspect about his previous criminal history on the videotape. If you have a special circumstance that makes it necessary to do so, you should do it after the initial interview has been concluded and a break exists in the videotape. This will avoid any editing problems for proper court presentation. Evidence such as a weapon or a shoe with a distinctive pattern, should also be videotaped separate from the interview in case the court later rules that such evidence is inadmissible.

REMINDERS

- No threats, no promises, no false statements.
- Ask one question at a time; make sure that it has been answered.
- Don't ask leading questions.
- Let the suspect finish his answer.
- Be patient; don't look at your watch.
- Don't let the second interrogator interrupt your questions.
- Don't discount irrelevant comments.
- Don't place too much value on inconsistencies.

- Don't reveal the extent of your knowledge.
- Don't hurry.
- Don't talk when you should be listening.
- Continue for another 15 minutes.

FINAL COMMENTS

Interrogation is not merely the use of techniques, there are many intangibles that are difficult to spell out. Techniques are something the beginner clutches on to, like the priest conducting his first baptism, he is constantly referring to his instructions to see what he should say next. Techniques limit your range of action. When you develop skill you draw on yourself, on your own experience of success and failure. You cull out those approaches that have been rewarding. You draw on your own imagination, on limitless material within yourself.

One is reminded of the taxi driver in Dublin who pulled up at a traffic light, looked around and then drove on. When his passenger complained that he had gone through a red light, the driver replied, " 'Tis a matter of philosophy, Sir. Traffic lights are there to help us, not to hinder us." Criminal interrogation is like driving a taxi in Dublin. You need to know the rules, but you don't have to obey them if there's a better way of getting to your destination.

Chapter 3
INTERVIEWING VICTIMS AND WITNESSES

What you don't see with your eye, don't witness with your mouth.

Yiddish Proverb

According to a Rand Corporation study of the criminal investigation process, the most important factor in determining whether a crime will be solved is the information provided by the victim or witness. Arrest and successful prosecution of a criminal often depends on the ability of police officers, to obtain detailed information from victims and witnesses. Police officers have to be able to talk to bank robbers and to bank presidents. Interviewing victims and witnesses requires the same skills as criminal interrogation.

There is the same need for quick assessment of character, rapid initiation of a cooperative relationship, and knowledge of the various ways of committing the crime under investigation. In short, you have to know what to ask and how to ask it. You also have to be ever vigilant, and on the watch at all times for inconsistencies. The victim or witness may become a suspect, and your interview becomes an interrogation.

Some victims and witnesses are excellent informants. All you have to do is to ask, "What happened" or "What did you see or hear?" Let the eyewitness talk, then ask a few questions to fill in any gaps in the account of the crime. Other eyewitnesses load you with information on unrelated events and give long-winded answers to your questions. Some people are not quick to volunteer information, which has to be drawn out of them. A few are not very observant and would have difficulty identifying Santa Claus.

Victims and witnesses who are not as helpful as one might wish should be interviewed in the police building. The familiar surroundings of their own neighborhood, home or office and the support of neighbors, family members or fellow employees may make it easier for them to avoid revealing information that they do not wish to share with the detective. On the other hand, they may be fearful of revealing information in the presence of these people, particularly neighbors.

When there are several witnesses at a crime scene, separate them, as a forceful, outspoken witness may influence the recollections of other less confident witnesses. When there are many witnesses, as for example at a shooting in a crowded bar, it is not a good idea to hand out statement forms like a pack of cards. Drunken tavern patrons are not usually highly motivated to assist the police. It is better to take aside a cooperative employee or customer and find out the names or descriptions of those who actually saw the shooting. The officers can concentrate their personal attention on these people.

Following a homicide at a drinking party a 19-year-old girl, who could not read, wrote on the police department witness statement form "i was walking don the steras." Two years later David reviewed the case records of this unsolved murder and sent a homicide detective to interview her. This time the detective wrote her account of the shooting, "I was with my boyfriend, Joe, we were sitting around in Joe's room getting high drinking beer and whiskey. Ray pulled a gun and was pointing it at everyone. Me and Joe got scared so we went downstairs to the kitchen to get something to eat.

"I heard a shot upstairs, me and Joe ran upstairs and saw Louie lying on the floor. Blood was coming from the right side of his head near his right eye. Ray was holding the gun in his hand and saying he didn't know there was a bullet in the gun. I think Joe called the police. The only reason I didn't say anything then was because I was afraid Ray would do something to me. I'm still afraid." The police questioned another person who was at the party and he confirmed the girl's account of the shooting. The suspect was arrested and pleaded guilty to second-degree murder.

Never use the word witness. This scares people. They have immediate dread of having to appear in court. Instead of saying, "Did you witness anything?" strike up a casual conversation and ask, "What happened?" Usually it is better to find out what a person knows before asking him for his name, address and driver's license or other identification.

David Powis, formerly a deputy assistant commissioner at Scotland Yard, emphasizes this approach. "In particular never, *never* ask for names and addresses until *after* the person has told you, in the form of general discussion and comment, conducted in friendly conversational tones, what he has seen. Then get *every* address and telephone number he has; work, home, and close relatives— even a neighbor's telephone number, where appropriate."

Avoid leading questions. If one witness tells you that an armed robber was wearing a blue coat, don't ask the next witness, "Was he wearing a blue coat?" Instead ask what he was wearing and the color. On estimates of height and weight, check the witness by asking him your height and weight. Separate facts from opinions. Always remember that your object is to find out what he knows. It is not to tell him what you know.

UNCOOPERATIVE VICTIMS AND WITNESSES

With a little effort the officer may be able to obtain significant help from uncooperative victims and witnesses, who tend to belong to the following types.

The Reluctant Witness

Some people do not want to spend time in court, and in order to avoid this they are reluctant to reveal information to police officers investigating a crime. Perhaps as a witness to another crime or traffic accident they had the experience of being required to appear in court time and again. Each time, after a long wait outside the courtroom, they were told that the defendant was successful in persuading the judge to delay the hearing until a later date.

Friends and relatives of the suspect, out of loyalty, may be reluctant to provide information. If, however, the police point out to a young woman that her boyfriend, the suspect, was stepping out on her, she may suddenly become cooperative. There are limits to family loyalty. Friends lose their sense of loyalty when they realize that they might become suspects themselves, or face arrest for providing false information to a police officer.

The Embarrassed Witness or Victim

Some people do not want anyone to know about their presence at a crime scene. They want to avoid either mention in the newspapers, or telephone calls to their home by the police. For example, the man who witnesses a robbery at a motel may have told his wife that he had to work overtime at the office, when in fact he was spending the evening in the motel with a girlfriend. The victim of a street robbery may be fearful of a newspaper report that he was robbed in an area frequented by male homosexual prostitutes.

Shortly after a tavern robbery, a patrolman questioned a couple in a car parked alongside the tavern. Instead of saying there had been an armed robbery inside the tavern and asking if they saw where the robbers went, the officer demanded to see the couple's identification. The demand aroused immediate anxiety because the man was with a lady who was not his wife. The result was that the officer did not get vital information on the getaway car.

The Dishonest Victim or Witness

Those victims who are themselves involved in illegal acts often are unwilling to give a completely truthful account of the crime to the police. For example, the owner of a small grocery store reports a robbery in which money was taken out of the cash register. In order to make a larger claim from his insurance company, he makes the false statement that the robber also forced him to open the safe. A man robbed at gunpoint in a drug deal may neglect to mention that he intended to buy an ounce of cocaine from the suspect. He reports only the robbery of $3,000 by a stranger.

The relatives of a man who had entered a plea of not guilty by reason of insanity to a charge of running a confidence game told John he was mentally ill. They reported that on several occasions in their presence, he had played Russian roulette. The manner in which the relatives described the suspect's previous history and behavior suggested an element of exaggeration. The above incident was, therefore, investigated more closely. It was found that the weapon was not a revolver but an automatic pistol. It is not possible to play Russian roulette with an automatic pistol, or else you play it once and die.

The Non-Victim Victim

The non-victim victim makes false reports of burglary, theft, armed robbery, sexual assault and other crimes. For example, a man who has lost his wages gambling does not want to admit this to his wife, so he calls the police to report that he was robbed in the street. He tells the patrolman that the suspect was wearing a red and white check jacket, which he later describes as black and white. This contradictory statement suggests the possibility of a false report, and alerts the officer to look for the other clues to false reports of armed robbery.

Very great distress on the part of a victim may distract the investigator's attention from discrepancies, or suspicious features in the victim's account of the crime. A woman, fearful of a severe beating by her husband, explains her late arrival home in the early hours of the morning by falsely claiming that she was kidnapped and raped. Her distress over the alleged rape appears to be genuine rather than simulated.

A young woman working alone at night in a donut store reported that she had been robbed at gunpoint. She was very distraught, sobbing and tearful. Indeed, it was difficult to calm her down so that she could talk to the officers. She had been so busy that she had not put money in the "drop safe" at intervals in accordance with store procedures. As a result, there was a lot of money in the cash register. In fact, she was living with speed freaks, she had hidden the money in the store, and she had made a false report of robbery.

When a victim is suffering from a gunshot or knife wound, concussion, or injuries from a bomb explosion, the possibility of a false report is likely to be overlooked. The man who reports that while walking across a park he kicked a can that exploded, may have been wounded by the explosion of a bomb that he made himself. The woman who reports that she was shot in the chest when she resisted the attempts of a burglar to rape her, may have shot herself in an attempt to commit suicide. A woman who has been stabbed by her husband may report that she was attacked by a stranger.

The motives for false reports, and the clues to recognition of these false reports, will be reviewed in later chapters. As in all interviews and interrogations: If you don't think of it, you won't look for it, and you won't find it.

The Anti-Police Victim or Witness

People, including victims, who do not like the police prefer not to help them in any way. Frank Gusenberg, the only victim still alive at the scene of the Saint Valentine's Day Massacre of members of the Bugs Moran gang in Chicago in 1929, was asked by the police who shot him. He replied, as he lay dying with 14 machine gun bullets in his body, "Nobody shot me." Even people who would not usually cooperate with the police may do so when the suspect is a sex offender. No one likes the thought that one's wife or children might be exposed to the risk of sexual assault.

Some of the techniques described in the previous chapter can be used to obtain the cooperation of these people. A witness at the scene of a suspected teen-age gang stabbing was asked by a homicide sergeant for her date of birth. She replied, "It's on there," referring to her ID, which she had provided. The sergeant paused and again asked, "What is your date of birth?" He did so without raising his voice or showing irritation. She gave him her birthdate. She was testing him and he established his control of the interview. After she signed her statement, he said, "What gang do you belong to? We won't write it down." She replied, "The Midnight Illusions."

The Macho-Victim

Some victims who would rather punish the offenders themselves may report the crime to the police but withhold information that might identify the suspect, or they may refuse to prosecute because they plan to take the law into their own hands.

The Fearful Victim or Witness

Those victims and witnesses who are fearful of retaliation by the criminal, may not cooperate with the police or the prosecutors. Often their first question is, "Will I have to testify in court?" You have to overcome their reluctance to provide information, and it may be possible for you to respond, "I hope it will never come to that. I'm going to put a case together so tight that I hope it will never come to trial." You can always point out that their testimony may save others from becoming victims.

Fear of retaliation is often a problem in high- crime rate neighborhoods. Rape offenders will often threaten to kill their victims if they report the crime. Fear of the Mafia also discourages cooperation with the police.

In New York in 1986, Romual Piecyk, a refrigeration engineer, lost his memory of being robbed after he got threatening telephone calls, found that the brakes on his van had been tampered with, and discovered that one of the robbers was a member of the Gambino crime family, one of the nation's most powerful Mafia groups. The 12-year-old son of this member of organized crime was killed in

1979 when struck by a car driven by a neighbor. Later, this neighbor mysteriously vanished. He is believed to have been murdered.

THE COGNITIVE INTERVIEW TECHNIQUE

Victims and witnesses may have difficulty in recalling the essential details of a crime, especially one that involves violence such as a rape, armed robbery, hit-and-run accident or homicide. It has been claimed that the cognitive interview technique is more effective in jogging memory than the traditional police interview, in which the victim or witness is asked to say in his own words what happened and is then asked specific questions to enhance the completeness of his report.

In the cognitive interview, four general memory-retrieval techniques are reviewed with the victim or witness.

Reconstruct the Circumstances

"Think about what the scene looked like—the rooms, the furniture, pictures on the wall or other items and the people or the street, the vehicles, the lighting, the weather and the people. How were you feeling and what were your reactions to the incident?"

Report Everything

"Don't leave anything out, even if you think it is some unimportant detail." Often vital information is recalled after thinking about unimportant details.

Recall the Events in Different Orders

This is done after the witness or victim has given the usual chronological account of the events. "Start with the thing that impressed you most in the incident. Go from there, forward and backward in time. Go through the incident in reverse order."

Change Perspective

"Place yourself in the role of a prominent character in the incident and think about what he or she must have seen."

After the narrative statement has been completed, the investigator uses specific prompts to obtain information. He asks the following questions:

Physical Appearance

"Did the suspect remind you of anyone? If so, why? Was there anything unusual about the suspect's physical appearance or clothing?"

Names

"If you think a name was spoken but you cannot remember it, try to think of the name's first letter. Go through the alphabet. Then try to think of the number of syllables."

Numbers

"Was a number involved? Was it high or low? How many digits did it have?"

Speech Characteristics

"Did a voice remind you of someone else's? If so, why? Was there anything unusual about it?"

Conversation

"What was your reaction to what was said? How did others react? Were there any unusual words or phrases?"

R.E. Geiselman and R.P. Fisher, authors of the 1985 National Institute of Justice Report, *Interviewing Victims and Witnesses of Crime*, note that some of these techniques have been used for many years. However, when all the techniques are used together, the interview effectively enhances eyewitness memory. They state that although cognitive and hypnosis procedures are equally effective, the former can be learned and applied with relatively little training, and its use takes less time than does hypnosis. Moreover, since 1979 many appellate courts have ruled against hypnotically elicited testimony.

EYEWITNESS IDENTIFICATION

Many defense lawyers take the position that eyewitness identification of suspects is of no value. Elizabeth Loftus, a professor of psychology at the University of Washington, is an outspoken critic of eyewitness testimony. She has testified in more than 90 trials in the United States, including the first trial of the alleged serial murderer Ted Bundy.

In murder trials involving eyewitness testimony, she testifies that the possibility of error increases with stress, violence and the passage of time. She reviews the difficulty many people have in identifying a member of another race; "weapon focus" where the witness's attention on the weapon leaves less time and capacity for noting and remembering other details; and "unconscious transference," which means the mistaken recollection or the confusion of a person seen in one situation with a person that has been seen in a different situation or context.

An example of "unconscious transference" occurred when a rape victim identified a man she saw in the street as the rapist. This man, a psychologist, was placed in a line-up and once again she identified him. However, he had an excellent alibi, on the night of the rape he appeared with the chief of police on a live television program on eyewitness identification. The rape victim had watched this program.

The research of Loftus is based on experiments in college classrooms. Whether a student in the comfort of a classroom makes an identification does not matter; there are no consequences. A staged event in a classroom is very different from a murder or armed robbery. In real life the witness is involved in a very unpleasant experience, his life may be in danger, and he has to take time off from work to go to court.

J.C. Yuille and J.L. Cutshall could not find any studies of real-life witnesses in the research literature. They left the classroom to study the memory of 13 witnesses who observed a shooting incident in which one person was killed and a second seriously injured. Their research on actual witnesses to a crime does not give credence to classroom findings that the possibility of error in the memory of witnesses increases with stress, violence and the passage of time.

The incident took place on a major thoroughfare in midafternoon. A man entered a gun shop, tied up the owner and left the store with money and guns. The store owner freed himself, picked up a revolver and went outside to get the license number of the robber's car. The robber, who had not gotten in his car, fired twice from about six feet, seriously wounding the store owner. The victim fired six times at the robber, killing him. People on the street, in passing cars, or in adjacent buildings witnessed various aspects of the incident.

The witnesses, who had all been interviewed by the police after the shootout, were interviewed again five months later. There was no rapid decline in their memory. There was little change in the amount or accuracy of their recall of the incident. The witnesses resisted leading questions, and their stress level at the time of the event appeared to have no negative effects on subsequent memory. The results, as reported in the *Journal of Applied Psychology* (May 1986), were very different from the classroom studies.

Judges will sometimes dismiss the testimony of a witness because some detail has been incorrectly recalled. These experts point out that their study shows that incorrect recall of a detail, such as the date of the event or the color of the suspect's clothing, is unrelated to the rest of the witness's account. Some colors are not remembered. Some people have difficulty estimating the age, height and weight of suspects, or the speed of vehicles, but these are perceptual problems not memory problems. Most people are not trained in these observational skills.

In court, a few psychological experts have been used to discredit eyewitnesses. More recent research by other psychologists, including Yuille, should be drawn to the attention of the court. The reliability of children as witnesses will be reviewed in Chapter 8 on rape and other sex offenses.

HYPNOSIS

Hypnosis has been used extensively in questioning victims and witnesses in major unsolved crimes. Memory recall under hypnosis may be inaccurate and misleading but sometimes valuable information has been obtained. In the Chowchilla, California, kidnapping in 1976 a school bus driver and 26 children were abducted at gunpoint. The victims were sealed in a remote rock quarry, but the driver and two of the older boys succeeded in digging their way out. The bus driver could not recall the license plate numbers of the vans used by the kidnappers, but under hypnosis he suddenly called out two license plate numbers. One of them, with the exception of a digit, matched the license plate number of a van driven by the kidnappers. This information expedited the solution of the case according to W.S. Kroger and R.G. Douce.

In another case, described by Kroger and Douce, the use of hypnosis resulted in the arrest and conviction of a sex offender who probably would not otherwise have been captured. He kidnapped two San Francisco-area girls aged seven and fifteen, telling them that the doors of his car were wired with an explosive device that he would trigger if stopped by the police. The girls were taken to Mexico, where the older girl was raped and sodomized in a motel room near the border. The girls were released with the warning that any disclosure would mean certain death to their parents. The older girl succeeded in identifying the motel room, but the suspect had registered under an assumed name.

Under hypnosis the older girl recalled additional information including a hilltop San Diego gas station, where the suspect used a credit card to pay for repairs. FBI agents located the gas station and identified the credit card transaction. The suspect, an ordained minister who was married and a father, was arrested in his home in northern California. The suspect's photo was recognized by other girls who had been sexually assaulted.

In recent years, courts in many states have banned the use in court of "hypnotically refreshed" eyewitness testimony. Dr. Martin T. Orne, the psychiatrist who showed that Kenneth Bianchi, the Hillside Strangler, was faking a multiple personality disorder while under hypnosis, makes the following points:

● Hypnosis is not a reliable method of ascertaining the truth.

- Actual memories cannot be distinguished from confabulations (fantasies) either by the subject or by the hypnotist without full and independent corroboration.
- A "memory" can be created in hypnosis where none existed before and such pseudomemories may come to be accepted by the subject as his actual recall of the original events. They are then remembered with great subjective certainty and reported with conviction.
- It is possible for an individual to feign hypnosis and deceive even highly experienced hypnotists.

The Council on Scientific Affairs of the American Medical Association reported that recollections obtained during hypnosis can involve confabulations and pseudomemories and not only fail to be more accurate, but actually appear to be less reliable than non-hypnotic recall.

Chapter 4
ASSESSMENT OF PERSONALITY

No change of circumstances can repair a defect of character.

Emerson, *Essays*

A detective within a few minutes of meeting a suspect, victim, or witness, has an impression of that person's character. This impression, that comes to mind almost instinctively, is based upon myriad observations. Often beyond conscious awareness, the detective's mind combines information already known about the person with the person's general appearance, clothing, tone of voice, choice of words and body language, as well as his response to the detective and to others. Rapid assessment of personality is a skill worth cultivating.

Profiles of the following personality types will be reviewed in this chapter: antisocial personality, hysterical personality, schizoid personality, paranoid personality and sadistic personality.

ANTISOCIAL PERSONALITY

There's a sure market for imposture.

Byron

Almost four out of five men sentenced to prison for felonies are antisocial personalities, according to S.B. Guze's *Criminality and*

Psychiatric Disorders. They are also called sociopathic or psychopathic personalities. We prefer the term sociopathic personality because it does seem uncharitable to saddle persons with the label antisocial when not all their behavior is antisocial. Sociopaths are impulsive, irresponsible, self-centered people who live as if there is no tomorrow. They care not for the social and legal restrictions of everyday life and resent those in authority, yet they like to boss other people.

They seem not to have a conscience and may commit the most brutal crimes without showing any feelings of guilt or remorse. Indeed, in the courtroom, a sociopath may laugh and joke about the callous, unprovoked, shotgun slaying of an elderly couple during a burglary in their home. A young armed robber, when informed of his father's death responded, "What else is new?" A few weeks later he shocked the penitentiary chaplain by reacting to news of his mother's death with the nonchalant inquiry, "Where's the insurance money?"

Sociopaths have difficulty holding a job unless it offers constant change and action with little direct supervision. The Army overseas in wartime; long distance truck driving (the wife has to take care of the children and he is relieved of many of the responsibilities that face fathers who live at home); and flying planes to smuggle drugs from South America are among the occupations that appeal to the sociopath. Some sociopaths do have good work records.

Although outwardly very independent, rebellious people, they are in fact very dependent on others. You can take advantage of their need for attention and respect in your interrogation. They make friends easily, but have difficulty maintaining friendships because they demand much and give little in return. A long-suffering wife may continue to support her sociopathic husband financially over many years of a stormy, troubled marriage.

Like a child called to account for some misdeed, the sociopath points the finger of blame elsewhere. Any failure in life, loss of a job, financial reverse, divorce, or arrest for a criminal act is attributed to an unjust employer, a heartless wife, incompetent teachers, unloving parents or society in general. Curiously, even though the sociopath may have good reason to blame his parents for childhood neglect or physical abuse, he may persist in speaking of them almost exclusively in loving and grateful terms. This may occur even though he has murdered one of them.

Those sociopaths with an impressive appearance, a gift of the gab and an ability to inspire confidence make good used car dealers and con artists. On the other hand, some sociopaths look disreputable and, far from inspiring confidence, create an immediate feeling of distrust. Even if his appearance is scruffy, he may still be able to fool others. A widely respected sheriff complained that he had been unable to cash a check in a store despite satisfactory identification, yet a sociopathic bad-check passer managed to do so despite his shabby clothing, inadequate identification and an out-of-state check.

The term manipulation is used to refer to the sociopath's skill in persuading others to do what he wants, whether through charm, flattery, fast-talk, promises, deceit, threats or arousal of feelings of guilt ("If you don't help me, I'll lose my job").

They tell the most outrageous lies without blinking, even when these lies serve no useful purpose. H.M. Cleckley gives this example in *The Mask of Sanity:* A sociopathic husband, already divorced by his wife, wrote in a letter to her matter-of-fact instructions about the insurance policies he was sending separately to provide for her and their children. There were no insurance policies and he had never seriously considered providing for his family in this way or any other. He was well aware that his lie would soon be found out, and he had nothing to gain materially by doing such a thing.

Disregard for the truth is not seen in their every statement. Despite their lack of conscience, not all their checks bounce, not all their promises remain unfulfilled, and at times they can show regard for the welfare of others. Some sociopaths are delightful rogues, full of good stories, and entertaining drinking companions, but don't invite them to your home, don't lend them any money and don't tell them about police investigations.

You should be aware that not all sociopaths have criminal records. The talented sociopath may be a police officer, doctor, teacher or senior Army officer. He may be on the board of directors rather than in the joint. The fact that someone is regarded as an outstanding citizen does not rule out the possibility that he is a sociopath and a possible suspect in the crime that you are investigating. He is the serial killer John Gacy who was photographed standing alongside Rosalynn Carter, when her husband was president. He is killer Ted Bundy, the law student who was a volunteer working for the re-election of the Republican governor of the state of Washington.

If you wonder whether someone is an antisocial personality, it is a good idea to ask him if he has had any trouble with the law, has he been in many fights, what is the most serious injury he has suffered in a fight, what is the most severe injury he has given to anyone in a fight, does he have difficulty holding a job, where did he first meet his wife, and how long did he know her before he married her? If he tells you that his wife is a stripper, and that he married her three days after meeting her in a topless bar, it may well be that he has a problem with impulsive behavior.

If you use the following checklist, keep in mind that the sociopath or antisocial personality will conceal information or provide false answers. For example, he may say he has held three jobs since leaving school. If you start with his first job listing his age and date of employment, and then move onto other jobs with age and date, you may find that he remembers 30 jobs. He tells you that he served two years in the Navy and reached the rank of petty officer, but his Navy records show that he was discharged within a year. All too often the claims of a sociopath are accepted at face value and the detective fails to identify a likely suspect.

Profile of the Antisocial Personality

- Usually male.
- Age 16 to 40, they tend to "burn out" as they grow older, but some institutionalized offenders commit crimes of violence in their 40s and 50s.
- Antisocial behavior.

- Arrest records may be for burglary, theft, check offenses, assault, DUI, drug offenses, armed robbery, sex crimes or murder. They help themselves to whatever is at hand, whether it is your car, your wallet or your wife.
- Irresponsibility, unreliability, but not all of the time.
- Impulsivity, but sometimes show surprising self-control.
- Disregard for the truth.
- Apparent absence of remorse, guilt or shame.
- Makes friends easily but fails to maintain stable personal relationships, lacks capacity for loving caring relationships.
- Early discharge from armed services.
- Poor work record, but may hold job with a lot of action.
- Failure to learn from experience, including punishment.
- Blames others for his misfortunes in life.
- Poor judgment, getaway car has empty gas tank, defends self in court.
- Outwardly very independent, but underlying dependency on others.
- Self-centered, immature, attention-seeking behavior.
- Appearance may be impressive (con man) *but* can look disreputable and far from inspiring confidence may create an immediate feeling of distrust.
- The talented antisocial personality is not in the joint but is on the board of directors.

When Juvenile Delinquents Become Antisocial Personalities

The antisocial personality does not begin his antisocial behavior in adult life, but among 500 children referred to a child guidance clinic because of antisocial behavior, only one-fourth became antisocial adults. In a comparison group of normal school children, only 2 percent became antisocial adults. The more antisocial symptoms—such as lying, stealing and truancy—a child showed, the more likely he was to become an antisocial adult. However, less than half of even the most antisocial children were diagnosed as antisocial personalities when followed up years later, according to Herbert Yahraes.

HYSTERICAL PERSONALITY

A picture of women in the words of men... a caricature of femininity.

Chodoff and Lyons

Many hysterical personalities are women, and many female prisoners have hysterical personalities, but felony convictions are not common among hysterics. Crime is largely a product of youth and masculinity, so women do not figure prominently in crime statistics. Women account for 11 percent of the arrests for violent crime and 24 percent of the arrests for property crime, according to the FBI. The hysterical personality tends to show dramatic, attention-seeking behavior. The female hysteric, like the male antisocial personality, is very manipulative, and she uses tears and sex to persuade men to meet her demands.

The dramatic displays of emotion may have great impact on people unfamiliar with this type of personality. Tears and sobbing may arouse sympathy, but the skilled observer will sense that the feelings lack depth. The hysteric, despite the extravagant display of emotion, does not seem to be severely depressed. In an instant, tears turn to light-hearted laughter. They can be very seductive. The blouse, which may be transparent, is poorly buttoned, and the dress is allowed to ride up so that a large expanse of thigh is exposed.

This hysterical female personality, whether victim, witness, confidential informant or suspect, may ask you to come to her apartment at night. She insists on seeing you alone and may say that she will only talk to you. She answers the door dressed in a nightgown or other inappropriate, skimpy clothing. You would be wise to excuse yourself and return with a partner. The more sophisticated hysterical personality is much more subtle in her efforts to compromise you in a sexual relationship.

Many of these women are strikingly attractive in their appearance, and this cannot always be attributed to skillful use of make-up and gifted selection of attire. The latter factors may compensate for deficiencies of nature and the inroads of advancing age. Gait and posture contribute to the overall impression of feminine charm. These women are always on the stage, and their behavior reflects the sophistication of their cultural background. They do not all show their exhibitionistic tendencies in revealing or otherwise provocative clothing. However, when they pull their dress down, they may do so in such a way as to defeat the ostensible purpose of modesty by lifting up the skirt before stretching it down over their knees.

The first time a hysterical personality meets you, she compliments you on your skill as a detective. Your first reaction is one of delight at meeting such an intelligent, perceptive witness, victim or suspect, but then you realize that she has done all the talking and you have hardly said a word. Then she starts criticizing other police officers. This should warn you of your danger. The hysterical personality starts off by flattering you; then when she finds she cannot obtain as much of your time as she wants, or cannot otherwise manipulate you, she turns against you. She telephones your supervisor or the chief of police to complain about you.

These people are very dependent, self-centered and insecure, who make great demands on your time and patience. They are not reliable informants. They tend to exaggerate and can be as untruthful as antisocial personalities. Threats of suicide are made to gain attention or to control husbands, lovers, employers and others. Suicidal gestures may be successful: they lean too far out of a window or misjudge the lethality of sleeping pills or the time of arrival home of a husband to turn off the gas. Here death is an accident in a dramatic setting.

Profile of the Hysterical Personality

- Usually female, tomboy in childhood; males are effeminate.
- Age 18 to 45.
- Criminal offenses include shoplifting, check and credit card offenses, prostitution, drug offenses, carrying a concealed weapon

(for male friend), homicide.

- Sexually provocative clothing, blouse unbuttoned to reveal breasts, or transparent blouse, low-cut dress.
- Seductive behavior, flirtatious, cross and uncross legs, panties visible at some time during interview, attachment to older men, sexually suggestive remarks.
- Dramatic attention-seeking behavior; suicidal threats, gestures or attempts.
- Volatile expression of emotions, use of tears to manipulate men, moods change rapidly.
- Emotional shallowness, feelings lack depth.
- Disregard for the truth, answers vague, exaggeration of stressful circumstances, sickness, injuries or whatever.
- Dependency, demanding behavior.
- Self-centered, vain, egocentric, immature.
- Flattery of persons in authority, followed by criticism and spiteful behavior.

SCHIZOID PERSONALITY

The awkward, shy, aloof, schizoid personality has difficulty in forming relationships and lives in a daydream world of his own fantasies. He avoids eye contact, has a limp handshake and a cold smile. He is very sensitive and may be suspicious of others. Some schizoid personalities never come to the attention of either the police or psychiatrists, but are thought to be strange and eccentric by their fellow employees and neighbors. Others lead a borderline existence on skid row and some become frankly schizophrenic. A peculiar blank stare and dishevelled look suggest the shift from personality disorder to schizophrenia.

Some severe schizoid personalities and schizophrenics wear ill-assorted clothes and carry sacks containing all manner of odd items. Detectives who stopped a man wearing two sets of clothes, asked John about this. The man had shown a Veteran's Administration hospital ID card, so John asked him just one question, "What was your doctor's diagnosis?" He replied, "I'm a dangerous paranoid schizophrenic." John moved on quickly. VA patients often know their diagnosis.

Profile of the Schizoid Personality

- Awkward, shy, aloof, eccentric.
- A loner, he has difficulty in forming social relationships.
- Limp handshake, cold smile.
- Very sensitive, suspicious of others.
- Some wear ill-assorted clothes, carry sacks containing odd items and lead a borderline existence on skid row.
- May have psychotic, schizophrenic episodes with hallucinations and delusions.
- May commit assault or murder; when the victim is a woman, sexual mutilation (post-mortem) is more likely to occur than rape.
- Remorse following brutal crime may lead to confession.

PARANOID PERSONALITY

In contrast to the schizoid personlity, the paranoid personality is more likely to achieve success at work, and he may have his own business or do well in some profession. He is also more likely to have a wife and family. Both his career and his home life may suffer from the consequences of his jaundiced outlook on life. The outstanding features of the paranoid personality are his suspiciousness and mistrust of others.

He is a humorless, rigid person, who is unwilling to compromise. Sensitive to slights, he is always expecting someone to take advantage of him, or to make fun of him. He makes mountains out of molehills. Often aggressive and resentful of discipline, he is tense, hypervigilant, and constantly expecting treachery. If married, he is very jealous. Suspecting his wife of infidelity, he checks her activities whenever she is away from home. Often he terrorizes her and their children.

The paranoid personality may become delusional and would then be diagnosed as suffering from a paranoid disorder or paranoid schizophrenia. Hallucinations and delusions, when they occur, are superimposed on the paranoid personality, and are not part of it. He becomes convinced that others are out to harm him, and he may even believe that there is a plot against his life. Yet he will not readily reveal his false beliefs to others. He may, however, complain to the police that his neighbors have threatened him or thrown garbage on his property.

Eventually his paranoid delusions will involve the police, the courts, and indeed anyone who questions his paranoid complaints. He may take the law into his own hands with fatal consequences for those he believes are against him. It has been said that if you put a mask over a person's face, leaving only the eyes visible, you could make a diagnosis of paranoid psychosis from the extremely paranoid look of the person's eyes.

Profile of the Paranoid Personality

- Cold, unemotional, rigid, humorless.
- Suspicious and mistrustful of others.
- Easily slighted, quick to take offense.
- Litigious.
- Extremely jealous of wife.
- Secretive.
- Blames others for his problems.

SADISTIC PERSONALITY

The sadist derives pleasure from inflicting pain or humiliation on others. He delights in cruelty. In childhood, other children or animals are the victims. Cats are killed, dogs are set afire, or a dog and a cat are tied by their tails and suspended from a clothesline with fatal outcome for both.

Fascination with fire is common from an early age. He not only plays with matches but also sets fires, which may reduce the family home to ashes. There is an old saying that children who play with fire will wet the bed. The adage does not say that children who wet the bed will play with fire. If this was true, our cities would have been reduced to ashes years ago. The triad of childhood cruelty to animals, firesetting and bedwetting may predict violent behavior.

In adult life, animals, children or adults are the victims. Sadism is often combined with sexual abnormalities such as impotence, indecent exposure, window peeping, obscene telephone calls and rape. The sadistic personality may have an extensive collection of pornographic magazines and women's underclothing, possibly stolen from clotheslines.

He may try to obtain employment that brings him in contact with the dead or dying, for example work as a meat cutter, a packing company employee who slaughters animals, a mortician, a morgue attendant, a paramedic, an operating room technician or a doctor. Fascination with firearms, explosives, martial arts and torture may be present. Watch also for a history of firesetting and employment as a firefighter or volunteer firefighter. The sadistic personality may refrain from the use of tobacco, alcohol and drugs. There may be a history in his childhood of parental physical abuse, sexual abuse or both.

Profile of The Sadistic Personality

- Usually male, age 18 to 45.
- Possible arrest record for carrying a concealed weapon, assault, impersonation of a police officer, burglary, indecent exposure, obscene telephone calls, sexual assault, arson, bombing, murder.
- Prior application for employment as police officer, security guard, firefighter or volunteer firefighter.
- Employment as security guard (may have been fired for unsatisfactory performance), gunsmith, demolition worker, construction worker, meat cutter, mortician, morgue attendant, paramedic, operating room technician, doctor or other occupation that brings him in contact with bloodshed and death.
- Fascination with firearms, fires, explosives, martial arts, blood

sports such as dogfighting using pit bull terriers, Nazi paraphernalia, torture, pornography, and S and M stores that sell whips, handcuffs, and leather restraints, as well as magazines and books that feature acts of sadism and masochism.

- Possession of handcuffs, spotlight on car that is like a standard unmarked police car and a mail order police badge or false police identification.
- History of parental physical abuse and sexual abuse, or awareness of abnormal parental sexual activity such as incest or promiscuity.
- Childhood cruelty to animals such as disembowelling pet rabbit, suspending cat and dog by their tails from clothesline, or placing cat in microwave oven so that it explodes.
- Childhood firesetting.
- Childhood bedwetting, which is significant only if accompanied by childhood firesetting and cruelty to animals. The cruelty to animals, firesetting and bedwetting may continue into adult life.
- Arson.
- Bombings.
- Sadistic acts, such as pistol whipping a cooperative robbery victim or repeatedly stabbing a rape victim.
- May be a respectable citizen in the opinion of his wife, employer and others who know him.

Chapter 5
NICKNAMES AND TATTOOS

Nicknames and whippings, when they are once laid on,
no one has discovered how to take off.
W.S. Landor, *Imaginary Conversations*

Both nicknames and tattoos can provide clues to the bearer's personality, but this is not their only value. When the name of a suspect is not known, knowledge of his nickname may lead to his identification. Tattoos are less useful, but occasionally contribute to a successful arrest. Nicknames and tattoos are usually recorded on contact cards and on the fingerprint cards of people arrested by the police. This information, especially on nicknames, is available in many police departments on either computer printouts or card index files. Interrogators should always ask suspects for their nicknames. When appropriate, victims and witnesses also can be asked for this information. Today's victim may be tomorrow's suspect.

NICKNAMES

A nickname is the heaviest stone that the devil can throw
at a man.

Hazlitt, *Essays*

A man can change the name that he receives at birth, but he cannot easily escape the nickname that is given to him later in life by those who know him. Childhood nicknames often persist throughout life. The bearer himself may not know, or claim not to know, the origins of his new name. It may come from his surname: for example, Barnard becomes *Barnyard*, Ramstetter becomes *The Ram*, and Tokarski becomes *Two Car Keys*. Often, people named Roads or Rhodes are called *Dusty*. A nickname is usually derived from a person's appearance, personality or behavior. An exploit (creditable or discreditable), disaster or other significant event in his life may also provide his new name.

Many nicknames roll easily off the tongue, for example, *Billy the Kid*. In two or three word nicknames, each word may have the same initial letter, such as *Lucky Luciano*, *Big Bill* and *Pretty Paul the Pimp*. Others rhyme, like *Crazy Larry* and *Fat Pat*. High drama is common, as in *Machine Gun Kelly*, *Dynamite Sam* and *Killer Burke*. Nicknames confer status, and those without them sometimes invent names for themselves. There may be a cruel twist to nicknames, especially those acquired in penitentiaries. Criminals are quick to recognize the strengths and weaknesses of their associates, and when a humiliating nickname is given to a man of violence, care is taken not to use it in his presence. Flattering nicknames, such as *mojo*, or leader, are sometimes given to "boss cons" within penitentiaries and to gang leaders. One such offender was proud of his title, *Moses*, which he considered to indicate that he was a leader of his people.

A wide range of nicknames provide information on personality and behavior; for example, *Animal*, *Misfit*, *Loser*, *Creep*, *Bad News*, *Bashful*, *Slick* (a successful "con man"), *Jimmie the Weasel* and *Snake* (treacherous), *Benny the Beast*, *Cheater*, *Rooster* (feisty), *Ram* (a leader or girl chaser), *Stallion*, *Cassanova*, *Mule* (a very stubborn man), *Possum* (acts dumb whenever questioned by the police), *Puff the Magic Dragon* (more bark than bite), *Freddie the Freeloader*, *Mushroom Mike* (likes mushrooms), *Jellybean* (always eating jelly beans), *Sleepy* (looks sleepy) and *Itchy Willy* (always scratching himself).

Crazy Joe is clearly regarded by his friends as mentally unstable. Nicknames such as *Bats, Batty, Dippy, Dopey, El Vato Loco, Frankenstein, Goofy, Jake the Flake, Loony, Mad Dog, Madman, Retarded Eddy, Rubberhead, Spaceman, Squirrel, Weird* and *Zombie* warn of psychiatric disorder and unpredictable, strange behavior. *No Mind* was illiterate. *Dumb Tom*, an appropriate nickname as it turned out, made the mistake of warning another biker that he was coming over to his home to beat him up. The intended victim greeted *Dumb Tom* with a fatal shotgun blast. *Paranoid Al*, a speed freak, had a very paranoid attitude resulting from his chronic abuse of speed.

A readiness to fight is reflected in such nicknames as *Scrapper Sam, Knuckles* and *Thumper*. Dangerous men have nicknames that suggest a quick temper, such as *Snap Cap*. A readiness to shoot others is indicated by *Bang-Bang, Shotgun* and *Triggerman*. A member of organized crime had the ominous nickname *The Little Mortician*. A criminal's favorite weapon or his use of a particular weapon in a much publicized crime may be recorded in a nickname such as *Frying Pan, Kicking Sam, Machete, Baseball, Ax Handle* and *Machine Gun Kelly*. *Blood* was forever pulling out his knife in a confrontation. Overly talkative people are called *Motor Mouth*. Well-known police informants receive nicknames such as *Walkie-Talkie, Squealer, Parakeet* (always singing), *Parrott, The Mouth* and *Bucketmouth*. *The Preacher* was always philosophizing. *Cricket* spoke with a raspy voice. Religious nicknames, such as *Saint* and *Angel*, seldom indicate any deep religious beliefs. *Bible Salesman* preaches religion to others, but does not practice what he preaches. *Altar Boy* was originally a monk in a seminary. *The Deacon* has a pontifical air and tells lies with a straight, sober appearance.

Physical handicaps give rise to nicknames such as *Wheelchair Charlie, Harelip Harry, Asthma, One Lung, Four Fingers, Diabetic Ernie, Quasimodo, The Humpback*, and *Cripple*. *Sidewinder* had a twisted body from an accident. *Crisp* had scars on his body from severe burns. People who neglect to wash themselves are given names such as *Skunk, Bob the Pig, Dirty Ernie, Rancid Rich* and *Filthy Bill*. Choice of clothing may be noted in nicknames, for example, *Lavender* preferred lavender-colored clothes.

Nicknames may provide clues to the appearance of a suspect. *Pine Cone* and *Tree* suggest a tall person. *Jumbo, Moose,* and *Tiny* are likely to be large men. *Gorilla* is probably heavy and brutish-looking, while *Pygmy, Midget* and *Chico* are small men. *The Undertaker* can be emaciated or have a reputation as a killer. *Bones* and *Soupbone* are likely to be gaunt, and *Ghost* is a thin, shadowy figure. *Friar Tuck* and *Duffel Bag* are probably chubby. *Furback* has much hair on his chest and back. *Chocolate* and *Eight Ball* indicate dark skin color.

Nicknames are particularly helpful in their portrayal of an unknown suspect's face. Who could overlook *Cyclops, One-Eyed Eddie, Popeye, June Bug* (bulging eyes) and *Fishface* (poor bone structure with prominent eyes). *Four-eyes* has thick glasses, and the *Bifocal Bandit* was an older armed robber with bifocal glasses. *Blind Boy* had a disfigurement in his eyes that gave him the appearance of blindness. He was employed by other criminals to case businesses before a burglary. With the aid of dark glasses and a white cane, he stood around like a blind man waiting for someone to meet him. *Tear Drops* had these tattoos under one eye.

The Cat had a sneaky look in his eyes. A large nose is indicated by *Anteater* and *Pinocchio;* large ears by *Ears, Big Ears, Dumbo, Floppy* and *Mickey Mouse;* and prominent teeth by *Fang, Rabbit* and *Saber Tooth.* One criminal was called *Fang,* not because of prominent eye teeth, but after he bit a police officer's ear. *Sunshine* was always smiling, and *Hog Jaw* had fat jowls. People with a facial resemblance to famous individuals or cartoon characters have nicknames such as *Hitler, Castro, Khrushchev* (bushy eyebrows), *Charlie Brown* and *Flintstone.* What a contrast there must be between *Craterface* and *Pretty Boy,* between *Shovelface* and *Babyface. Baby Doll* had no blemishes. *Scarface* surely has a disfiguring scar that could not go unnoticed.

The size and shape of the head are indicated by nicknames such as *Pinhead, Light Bulb, Cue Ball, Hook Head* (deformed), *Parrot* (this man's head showed a striking resemblance to a parrot) and *Dog Head* (unkempt appearance). Red-haired people are called *Red,*

Red Dog and *Tomato Head*. *Golden Boy* is fair-haired, *Silver Fox* has prematurely gray hair, *Whitey Jones*, although young, has snow-white hair, *Harpo* has frizzy hair like Harpo Marx and *Haircut* acquired his name because of his poor, homemade haircut. *Caveman* has a beard, long hair and a generally shaggy appearance, as if he had just stepped out of a cave. Bald people have been called *Cue Ball* and *Light Bulb*. *Willie the Hat* always wears a hat.

Buzzard has a long neck with a prominent Adam's apple, and while waiting at an institutional chow line, he would sit perched on a railing mooching cigarettes. *The Duke* received his nickname from large diamond rings on his fingers, and *Flipper* was sensitive about his small hands, which he always kept in his pockets. Men with large feet are called *Bigfoot*, *Bigfeet* and *Bear Tracks;* those with long legs are known as *Spider*, *Spiderman* and *Grasshopper*. The slow walker is called *Turtle*, the man who runs fast, *Bullet*, and those with shuffling gait, *Penguin* or *Duck*.

Ethnic nicknames include *Chopsticks* for a man who had slanted eyes and an Oriental appearance. *Cherokee* looks like an *Indian*, *Little Israel* is Jewish and *Persian Joe* is an Arab. Nicknames can be a guide to a suspect's car such as *Cadillac* and *Mercedes;* to his birthplace, as in *Swiss Otto* and the *Saratoga Kid;* and to his occupation. *Milkman*, for example, drove a milk truck. *Gutter-Putter Mike* worked on gutters, and *The Barber* was a barber while in the state penitentiary.

An offender's favored criminal activity may be revealed by his nickname. *Stereo Slim* is a tall, thin burglar who specializes in the theft of stereophonic equipment. *Stinger*, another burglar, was arrested in a police "sting" operation. *Tippin Teddy* used to tiptoe into the bedrooms of his victims and snatch their belongings while they were sleeping. *Fast Eddy* was noted for his speed in obtaining stolen merchandise for his customers. Whether it was a blue suit, size 40, or a special type and size of snow tires, he would deliver the items within three or four days. *Radar* used to steal electronic equipment. *Pockets* is a pickpocket, *Shopping Bag* a shoplifter, and *ID Lady* is a check offender. *Candyman, Cocaine Man, John the Snowman, Speedball, Speed, Crystal, Crank* and *Junkie John* are all drug dealers. *Kilo* received his nickname after he was arrested with this amount of heroin in his possession. *Peashooter* is a trucker who sells fake amphetamines. Criminals involved in auto theft gangs have nicknames such as *Numbers* for specializing in the alteration of vehicle identification numbers, *Chopper* for working in a chop shop and *Wrench* or *Crescent* for skill in dismantling stolen vehicles.

Pervert is clearly a sexual offender. *Ester the Molester* and *The Leech* sexually assaulted children. A man accused of sodomy indignantly replied "You think I'd do a thing like that?" A check of his police record showed the nickname *Blackie Worm Hole. Barracuda*, a female offender when faced with arrest always offered to perform fellatio. *Fluff* is a homosexual prostitute. *Debbie the Dyke* is gay. The nickname *Pretty Paul the Pimp* provides a guide to both the suspect's appearance and his source of income.

Dynamite Sam, Sticks and *Stubs* are all bombers. *Stubs* derived his nickname from the loss of the tips of his fingers in the premature explosion of one of his devices. Arsonists have been called *Sparks*, *Sparky*, and *Firebug. Boxcar Jim, Freight-train Sam* and *Gondola Pete* are tramps who ride the rails. Gamblers have such nicknames as *The Bookie* and *Black Jack*, bootleggers *White Lightning* and muggers *Dark Alley Jim*.

Exploits in a criminal's career may be memorialized in a nickname. One man received the nickname *Checkers* after a young lady provided an alibi for him. She said she had spent the night with him. When asked on cross-examination what she was doing with him, she replied, "Playing checkers," an answer that was received with some skepticism. In a gambling raid, *Snookey the Mole* hid under a house in a crawl space and pulled dirt over himself. *Oarless* took a boat out on a lake, but the boat had no oars.

An officer's knowlege of the origin of a nickname flatters a suspect, and may make it easier for the officer to obtain information from him. *Rolaids* was proud of his nickname, which was given to him after a shootout that ended when he reached into his pocket for another shotgun shell and pulled out a roll of antacid.

The offender who is not proud of his nickname resents any reference to it.

TATTOOS

Of all the various motives for bearing a tattoo, the quest for personal identity is central.

G.W. Grumet

Tattoos are a declaration of identity (name, initials, penitentiary or social security number); group membership (insignia of armed services; outlaw motorcycle club or other gang); self-image *(Misfit, Unlucky, Reject, Zero, Born to Lose)*; religious beliefs (crucifix, hands clasped in prayer); standards of behavior *(Death Before Dishonor)*; emotional attachments (name or initials of mother or girlfriend surrounded by a heart, perhaps with an arrow through it or above *True Love)*; sexual interests (heterosexual or homosexual) and antisocial tendencies *(I hate cops)*.

Messages such as *Born to Kill* and *Jack the Ripper* may be designed to shock people, but they may also be prophetic. Richard Speck, who murdered eight nurses in Chicago, had the tattoo *Born to Raise Hell* on his left forearm. Some messages are misleading. In a study in the *Journal of Social Therapy*, Haines and Huffman found that those Illinois prison inmates with the tattoo *Death Before Dishonor*, who had been in the armed services, had all been discharged under conditions other than honorable. Some criminals with this tattoo are quick to provide information on partners in crime.

Pornographic pictures are common. Male homosexual prostitutes may have a tattooed arrow leading to the anus with messages on the buttocks such as *For Men Only* or *Open All Night*. Female prostitutes may have tattoos on the abdomen stating *Pay As You Enter, Danger Zone, Keep Off the Grass* or the price of sexual favors. Obscene tattoos are sometimes on the right arm, whereas religious tattoos, such as the cross or the Virgin Mary, are on the left arm. Bizarre tattoos with strange messages in unusual locations such as the abdomen or the inside of the wrist suggest a delusional mental illness such as schizophrenia.

When a suspect questioned on the street gives a name that does not match the tattooed initials readily visible on his forearm, there is reason to doubt whether he is being truthful. If he states he is staying with his aunt, a telephone call to her may reveal that she has a nephew with a name matching the initials on the tattoo and a body build similar to that of the suspect. When an NCIC check shows that her nephew is wanted for some crime, it becomes clear why he gave a false name and false identification.

Signs of the zodiac provide a clue to a person's date of birth. If a suspect with *Pisces* tattooed on his forearm provides identification showing a birthdate of December 12, he may well have false identification, because *Pisces* indicates birth between February 19 and March 20. The numbers *666*—The Sign of the Beast, a pentagram, an upside down cross, the letters SIL (Satan is Lord), the letter S with a line through it inside a circle (kissed or blessed by Satan), a clenched hand with the second and fifth fingers extended (the Satanic salute) or a goat's head suggest membership in a Satanic cult.

Members of outlaw motorcycle gangs do not always appear on the street bearded, unwashed, in a sleeveless jean jacket with their colors, motorcycle chain belt and engineer boots. It is important to quickly identify these people because of their tendency to carry concealed weapons and their dangerousness. Even one tattoo may betray their identity. Biker tattoos include *FTW* (fornicate the world), *HD Forever* (Harley-Davidson forever), *Live to Ride, Ride to Live, BTBF* (Bikers together, bikers forever), *DFFL* (Dope forever, forever loaded) and *BFFB* (Bandidos forever, forever Bandidos). Other gangs have their initials before and after the letters *FF*.

Numbers include *69, 13* and *1 percent*. The four major outlaw biker gangs: the *Hell's Angels, Bandidos, Pagans* and *Outlaws* do not approve of bikers from other clubs using the symbol *1 percent*. The Harley-Davidson emblem is commonly encountered, and one biker had it tattooed across the top of his bald head. The wings may have different colors signifying some perverse sexual act; for example, brown wings indicate oral-anal sexual contact. One biker had *God rides a Harley* tattooed on his penis.

After a five-year membership, the full colors of the gang can be tattooed across the back of the chest, and are referred to as the backpack. Club tattoos remain the property of the club, and if a member leaves without permission or if he provides information to the police, the biker tattoos can be removed. The club's enforcer either cuts off the tattoos or burns them off with a hot iron. A biker's old lady may have a butterfly tattoo on her breast, and *Property of* together with the name of the biker she belongs to, tattooed on her buttocks.

The "Pachuko" tattoo, a cross surrounded by dots between the thumb and forefinger was originally reported in West Coast youthful Chicano gang members. Fashions change, and many youth gangs have their own insignia or initials. A teardrop tattoo below the corner of the eye indicates five years in prison. Cuban criminals may have Cuban prison tattoos that show their crimes. A man with four dots between his thumb and forefinger has been convicted of murder. An armed robber has three dots and a thief two dots. An executioner has a heart with the word Madre inside it. A drug dealer has a triangle with a line through it and below it. A kidnapper has three lines coming to a point with a star beneath.

When the victim or witnesses report that the offender had a tattoo, or when a surveillance camera in a bank shows a tattoo, it becomes possible to distinguish between look-alike suspects. In a series of armed robberies, it was reported that the robber had two dice and the number 7 tattooed on the back of his hand. This information was a decisive factor in the criminal investigation.

Tattoos performed in penitentiaries are often poorly drawn, incomplete or have misspelled words. People with such tattoos, who claim that they have never served time, may not be reliable informants. Tattoos on the inner surfaces of the arms and elbows are sometimes designed to hide needle tracks from the intravenous injection of herion, amphetamines or other drugs, but a careful search may reveal these clues to drug addiction.

Chapter 6
HOMICIDE AND ASSAULT

Truth will come to light; murder cannot be hid long.
Shakespeare, *Merchant of Venice*

In murder, unlike many other crimes such as robbery, rape, burglary and arson, there is usually a prior relationship between the offender and his victim. A major focus in most homicide investigations and in most homicide interrogations is, therefore, on the offender-victim relationship. From 60 to 80 percent of all murders are committed by relatives or persons acquainted with the victims. Almost one in five of all killings involve family relationships, and one half of murders within the family involve spouse killing spouse.

There are so many motives for murder, so many methods of murder, and so many different circumstances of murder, that the interrogator's approach may well vary from one murder to the next. In general, however, the interrogation will usually begin with the strong, confident approach already described in Chapter 2. This can lead into: "We know what happened, we want to know why it happened. There's always a reason, it may not be a good reason, but there's always a reason," or "We have talked to others, and they've told us certain things, but we want to hear your side, your account of what happened."

Every effort should be made to obtain a confession before asking questions that are in the nature of excuses for the crime. Confessions can be facilitated by questions such as "Did you really intend to kill her? You didn't plan this, did you? I don't think you planned this, was it in the heat of passion? Did he push you too hard? Did he take advantage of you? Would this have happened if you hadn't been drinking?" Such confessions are of great value, and often other evidence shows that the crime was carefully planned rather than in the heat of passion.

In victim-precipitated homicides, which account for one-quarter to one-third of all homicides, the victim is the first to show and use a deadly weapon or to strike a blow in an altercation. In these victim-precipitated homicides, the victim is more likely to have a criminal record than the offender. It is often legitimate, therefore, to ask whether the victim was the first to resort to violence. "Did he threaten you? Were you afraid of him? Why?"

Sometimes a softer approach is indicated, in which there is a long, preliminary inquiry into the suspect's relationship with his victim, starting with, "When did you first meet him?" or "How long have you known him?" "Have there been any prior arguments, confrontations, threats, including homicidal threats, or fights? Has there been a sexual relationship, perhaps homosexual advances?" Inquiries are made to see whether the suspect will gain or will lose something because of the victim's death.

In his questions the detective will cover all aspects of the homicide. He will want to know when the suspect first obtained the weapon, where he obtained it and why. Did he have to go and get it, or does he carry it at all times? If he purchased it for target shooting, why did he buy hollow-point bullets? Did he test-fire the weapon on the day of the crime and if so, why? His answers to some of these questions may show premeditation. Was he ever at the scene of the crime; when was he last there; was he there on the day of the homicide?

How did he feel at the time of the homicide; was he under the influence of alcohol or drugs; how much alcohol had he taken; over what period of time; how did this affect him; what drugs had he used? Had he taken that amount of alcohol or drugs previously. Had he taken any medication prescribed by a doctor or any "over-the-counter" pharmacy drugs?

Ask him to describe the crime scene in great detail. His observations may show that he was very observant and had a good memory for what he saw. Such recollections throw doubt on claims of major alcohol or drug intoxication. Ask also about any stresses in his life at the time of the crime. Ask also about any prior loss of self-control or acts of violence for whatever reason. This information may be of value in showing that the homicide was not an isolated act of violence.

Did he take anything from the victim or from the crime scene? Did he return any such item to the victim's family? Did he return later to the crime scene, attend the victim's funeral or visit the victim's grave? If there was a search for the victim's body, was he one of the volunteers assisting the police in the search?

Even if the suspect protests his innocence, his detailed account of his activities on the day of the murder, his presence or absence at the scene of the crime, and his prior relationship with the victim may later prove of value because of statements that can be shown to be untrue.

Robert Ressler and other FBI experts have found that when someone outright denied they had murdered or had anything to do with the crime, the use of an imaginary third person was helpful. Agents would go through the details of the crime and ask the subject why he thought the third person would commit such an act. This technique projected responsibility away from the subject and onto someone else. The example was given of a murderer who provided a reason (sexual inadequacy) for the crime being committed.

Agent: Suppose we do it this way. Let's just divorce you from that situation. I'm sure you've thought about it a lot. Suppose it wasn't you involved and it was someone else. What, in your mind, would be the reasons for someone doing something like that?

Subject: I'd say she either said or did something extremely wrong.

Agent: Like what, for instance?

Subject: Well, it could have been that his (sexual) performance was inadequate. She might have thought it was. Or he might have thought it was and she said something about it (*FBI Law Enforcement Bulletin*, August 1985).

When sex is a factor, the offender may be unwilling to admit the homicide because of his fear that his sexual problems will become public knowledge, as in the following example of a homosexual murderer. David was successful in obtaining a confession.

An effeminate, young male homosexual was arrested in possession of a car belonging to an elderly single man who had been found stabbed to death in his apartment. He claimed that a friend of his had loaned him the car but he admitted knowing the victim. His story was that the older man gave him a ride in his car and took him to his apartment. When the man asked him to take part in a homosexual act, he left the apartment. He claimed that he was upset over the sexual advances, but he was picked up in an area frequented by homosexual prostitutes.

The detective told him "You're going to lie to me, deny that you know anything about his death. I'm going to testify in court, I find him dead, two days later you're caught driving his car. Initially everyone lies. Later on you'll say 'I did it, but this is how it happened.' The jurors may doubt your sincerity. The jurors will listen to what I'll say. Jurors would think about remorse, yet there are lies, lies, lies and then another story. Now's the time to tell how it happened.

"If we find your prints in the apartment, if people ID your picture and say they saw you leave the apartment you will be in trouble. Cold-hearted people deny, deny; they might believe someone who is remorseful." Eventually he confessed, but claimed that he was "high." The detective then questioned him at length about the room. His detailed observations showed that he clearly had his wits about him and was not in a state of drug intoxication.

When a shooting occurs outside a home where there is a drinking party and everyone denies knowledge of the homicide, then everyone at the party becomes a suspect. The investigating detectives are faced with the problem of questioning many people. When David had to question 20 people who had been at a party, he interviewed each person very briefly at police headquarters, asking only a few questions, including "What time did you arrive at the party?" and "Did you see anyone with a gun at the party?"

He concentrated on the first person who repeated one of his

questions. Almost certainly he was lying or concealing information. This man, instead of giving the time he arrived at the party, said, "What time did I arrive at the party?" On further questioning he revealed the name of a guest who left the party armed with a derringer to go after a stranger who had shot at another guest in an alley behind the house. The man with the derringer confessed to the homicide.

PROFILES OF MURDERERS

Murderers include a wide variety of people from the jealous husband to the Mafia hit man, from the wino on skid row who kills another derelict in an argument over a bottle of wine to the drug dealer who gives a "hot shot" to a nonpaying customer, and from the terrorist bomber who kills people he does not know to the mother who pours scalding water over her baby. Some murderers tend to fit a profile, and interrogators should keep likely profiles in mind when questioning suspects. The more features the suspect has of a particular profile, the greater the chance of his involvement in the crime.

Profiles are based on such factors as the offender's choice of victim, his method of committing the crime, his actions at the crime scene, his behavior after the crime, his childhood background, his personality and his lifestyle. Indeed, any aspect of his life may come under scrutiny. Special Agents of the Behavioral Science Unit of the FBI Academy, after interviewing 36 convicted sexual murderers, including 25 serial murderers, formed profiles of organized and disorganized murderers. The profiles given below have been adapted from their report and modified (*FBI Law Enforcement Bulletin*, August 1985).

Profile of the Organized Murderer

- Average to above-average intelligence, high school graduate or beyond.

- Socially competent, good appearance, neat dresser, may have designer clothes.
- Skilled work preferred, possibly security guard, often works at jobs below abilities, work history sporadic.
- Mobility with car in good condition; macho vehicle, sports car or four-wheel-drive pickup.
- Sexually competent.
- Living with partner.
- High birth-order status, often first-born son.
- Father's work stable.
- Inconsistent childhood discipline.
- Controlled, calm mood during crime, angry or depressed before crime.
- Use of alcohol with crime.
- Precipitating situational stress, problems with money, work or women.
- Planned offense.
- Victim a targeted stranger, may choose victims of similar appearance, occupation or lifestyle.
- Personalizes victim, tries to gain confidence of victim.
- In later conversation controls victim, gives orders and makes demands.
- Crime scene reflects overall control.
- Demands submissive victim.
- Restraints used; rope, chain, tape, belt, clothing, chemical, handcuff, gag or blindfold.
- Aggressive acts prior to death such as torture and rape.
- Body hidden.
- Brings own weapon, avoids leaving any physical evidence behind.
- Transports victim or body.
- Follows crime in news media, keeps news clippings.
- May change jobs or leave town after homicide, little or no remorse, may kill again, may involve himself in the police investigation, help search for the body.

Profile of the Disorganized Murderer

- Below-average intelligence, school dropout or marginal student.
- Socially inadequate, sloppy dresser, loner, may have delusional beliefs, may stutter, have acne, harelip or limp that contributes to poor self-image.
- Unskilled work, menial job, often unemployed.
- Has no vehicle, lives or works near crime scene.
- Sexually incompetent, often no sexual experience, never married.
- Living alone in rental property or with parents.
- Low birth-order status.
- Father's work unstable.
- Harsh discipline as child.
- Anxious mood during crime.
- Minimal use of alcohol.
- Minimal situational stress.
- Spontaneous offense, unplanned quality to crime scene.
- Victim/location known, but victim may be complete stranger; age and sex of victim do not necessarily matter.
- Depersonalizes victim, extreme brutality, assault to face, bite marks, post-mortem disembowelling, mutilation, urination or defecation on victim.
- Minimal conversation, possibly just orders and threats or no conversation at all.
- Crime scene random and sloppy, blood smearing, may drink or collect victim's blood, possibly ring of blood where he placed the container.
- Sudden violence to victim, quick death.
- Minimal use of restraints.
- Sexual acts after death, masturbation, ejaculation into stab wound or onto victim's clothing.
- Body left in view.
- Evidence often present, weapon, fingerprints, footprints. Weapon often one of opportunity, found at or near the crime scene, for example large rock or knife. Rarely uses firearms.

- Body left at death scene.
- Minimal interest in news media reports on the crime.
- Significant behavior change—drug or alcohol abuse, religiosity—after homicide. Remorse may lead to confession, less likely to kill again.

INTERVIEWING SERIAL MURDERERS

Serial killers suspected of contributing regularly each year to the homicide statistics deserve special attention. The sooner these people are behind bars, the better, and it is well worth the effort to do things for them that one would not dream of doing for run-of-the-mill thugs. Those who would criticize the following suggestions as unrealistic, would do well to keep in mind the stakes involved. Although the ideas come from a special agent of the FBI, which is well funded, even small police departments can obtain the necessary help from cooperative businessmen in an emergency.

First and foremost, one should stroke the ego of the suspect. He should be picked up for questioning in a large police car, equipped with more than one radio antenna, driven by a sergeant in police uniform. The interview should take place at night in a neutral location, perhaps a motel room or a room in a warehouse. There should be file cabinets to suggest that this is a special command post for this investigation. A critical piece of evidence should be placed at 90 degrees to the right or left of the suspect. His reaction on first seeing this evidence may add to the self-confidence of the interviewer.

The lead interviewer should clearly be someone special. Everybody defers to him, even the older, senior command officer shows respect on his visit to the command post. The message is clear — it took the best officers and a task force to capture the suspect, and now he is being questioned by the best interrogator. The magnitude of the investigation is made obvious to the suspect. The interrogator will support the suspect's philosophy that the victims were worthless objects. "They were whores, but we've got to investigate." He should take care not to refer to any of the victims as young. He should not mention their age or make any reference to child prostitutes.

If the suspect wants to write about his offenses, the officer will provide lined paper for the organized offender and unlined paper for the disorganized offender. If necessary, the suspect will be allowed to talk in the third person, and the interviewer will ask such questions as: "How do you think this guy got her in his car?"

If the suspect gets upset, the interviewer should not press for minute details. If the suspect does not like being asked about victim 3, the interviewer will move on quickly to victim 4. It is not wise to force an issue and thereby set up an adversarial situation. Face-saving explanations are supported. The suspect should not be asked about a subordinate accomplice, as he will get a message to this accomplice to destroy incriminating evidence as soon as he realizes that the police know about his accomplice. One should always be prepared for a marathon interview.

THE SADISTIC MURDERER

As long ago as 1911, Hans Gross, the German criminal psychologist, warned that "it will be well, in the examination of a person accused of a cruel crime, not to neglect the question of his sexual habits; or better still, to be sure to inquire particularly whether the whole situation of the crime was not sexual in nature." In a sadistic murder there may be no sexual assault and the sexual aspect of the offense passes unnoticed. Yet the murderer may have obtained a sexual thrill, perhaps even orgasm, from stabbing the victim so that he is no longer interested in any possible plan for sexual assault.

In the background of sadistic murderers, one looks for a childhood history of sex related to violence. For example, a brutal father who beats and sexually assaults his children, his wife or other women. Levin and Fox, in their book on mass murder, stated, "A set of childhood characteristics held by many to be associated with violent behavior has been named the 'Macdonald triad,' after psychiatrist John M. Macdonald, who first suggested the possibility that three

factors could predict violent behavior." The three factors in childhood histories are firesetting, extreme cruelty to animals and bedwetting.

John doubts that he was the first to suggest the importance of
these three factors that often seem to go together. Nevertheless,
the factors are found with surprising frequency in sadistic murderers. The cruelty is indeed extreme, for example disembowelling a
pet rabbit. It may be combined with firesetting, for example throwing gasoline on a dog and then setting it alight, or bombing, for
example catching a large fish, placing a cherry bomb in its mouth,
throwing it back in the water and watching for the explosion. The
bedwetting tends to be severe, but like the other two factors is
often concealed so that the triad does not come to light unless the
patient is questioned skillfully. Sometimes the information is only
forthcoming from relatives.

Do not ask a suspect if he has set fires; instead, ask him whether
he played with matches as a child, liked to hang around fire stations,
accidentally caused any fires, set trash fires, set fire to any aban-
doned shacks or empty buildings. Do not start with movie theaters
and hotels. The full range of questions for a suspected firesetter is
given in Chapter 11.

Similarly, do not ask a man if he has ever been cruel to animals.
This is "un-American" behavior and will be denied. It is better to
ask whether as a child he had any pets. Did he have to discipline
them? Then ask for example, if there are any animals he dislikes.
If so, what has he done to them? These men may feel comfortable
revealing acts of cruelty to disobedient dogs or to snakes, cats, fish
or other animals that they dislike, providing one does not ask about
cruelty to animals.

Always ask about the clothesline trick, in which a cat and a dog
are tied by their tails and suspended from a clothesline. The cat
will disembowel the dog, which will bite the cat to death. If the
suspect denies such activity, ask him if he has ever seen anyone
else do it. If he has seen his best friend do it several times, can
there be any doubt about his sadistic interests?

Questions about bedwetting in childhood might appear to have no place in a homicide investigation. However, the suspect with the childhood triad who is asked this question must have an uncomfortable feeling that the detective can read his mind. Often the bedwetting is a major problem, which may extend into adult life. Many children wet the bed, but few of them are firesetters and cruel to animals. It is the presence of at least one of the other two factors that prompts the inquiry.

Similarly, many psychologically healthy citizens become police officers, firefighters, doctors, paramedics or morticians, and may collect firearms, as well as Nazi memorabilia. Their choice of profession or hobby only becomes significant when associated with sadistic interests. Keep this in mind when reviewing the profile of the sadistic murderer.

Profile of the Sadistic Murderer

- Usually male, age 16 to 45.
- Arrest record for carrying a concealed weapon, assault, impersonation of a police officer, burglary, indecent exposure, obscene telephone calls, sexual assault, arson, bombing, murder. There may be no previous arrests, yet one or more of the above offenses may have been committed.
- Prior application for employment as police officer, security guard, firefighter or volunteer firefighter.
- Employment as security guard (may have been fired for unsatisfactory performance), gunsmith, demolition worker, construction worker, meat cutter, mortician, morgue attendant, paramedic, operating room technician, doctor or other occupation that brings him in contact with firearms, explosives, bloodshed or death.
- Fascination with firearms, fires, explosives, martial arts, blood sports such as dogfighting using pit bull terriers, Nazi paraphernalia, torture, pornography, and S and M stores that sell whips, handcuffs and leather restraints, as well as magazines and books that feature acts of sadism and masochism.
- Possession of handcuffs or other restraints, spotlight on car that

is like a standard unmarked police car and a mail-order police badge or false police identification.

- History of parental physical abuse and sexual abuse or awareness of abnormal parental sexual activity such as incest or promiscuity.
- Childhood cruelty to animals such as disembowelling pet rabbit, suspending cat and dog by their tails from clothesline, or placing cat in microwave oven so that it explodes.
- Childhood firesetting.
- Childhood bedwetting, which is significant only if accompanied by childhood firesetting and cruelty to animals. The cruelty to animals, firesetting and bedwetting may continue into adult life.
- Arson.
- Bombings.
- Sadistic acts, such as tightening and loosening cord around victim's neck to watch victim become unconscious, repeatedly stabbing a rape victim, or torturing a victim and recording the victim's screams on an audio or video recorder.
- May be a respectable citizen in the opinion of his wife, employer and others who know him.

An example of the usefulness of this profile was provided by the use of it in questioning a young woman, charged with the sadistic murder of a casual acquaintance.

- Female, in her 20s. As a woman she did not fit the profile, which lists the sadistic murderer as a man.
- Arrest record for carrying a concealed weapon, assault including assault of a police officer, resisting arrest, petty theft and driving under the influence of alcohol. She had sexually assaulted other women ("fist fucking"), but had not been arrested for these offenses.
- She did not fit the profile, as she had not previously applied for work as a police officer, security guard, or firefighter.
- At one time she wanted to become a mortician. She did not want to become a paramedic but she liked to drive to the scenes of auto accidents reported on the radio, in order to see the bloodshed.

- Firearms were not an important factor in her life, but before the murder she carried a .38-caliber revolver and 40 hollow-point bullets in her pockets. She was fascinated by fires, and as a child she liked to blow up aerosol cans.
- Possession of handcuffs and leather restraints.
- Physical and sexual abuse by relatives in her childhood.
- Childhood cruelty to animals including cutting the heads and legs off lizards, hanging a kitten, stabbing a pet cat and two pet dogs to death, then cutting off the head and legs.
- Childhood firesetting. Initially she denied firesetting, but on further questioning she revealed that she she had been accused of burning two homes that belonged to her parents. She also admitted that while she was burning garbage, her parent's new car was destroyed by fire.
- Bedwetting was a problem until she was eight years of age.
- Arson. She said that she might have set a fire in a building the night she had attended a meeting in the building, and was relieved to hear that the police said it was an accidental fire. Her roommate suspected her of setting fire to the car of the roommate's former husband. She was jealous of this man's relationship with her roommate. Before the murder she had been burning clothes and the plastic caps of bottles. Her roommate told her that she had an obsession with fire and that it was not safe in the house.
- Bombing. She was given a medical discharge from the Air Force after she threatened to blow up her squadron.
- Sadistic acts. She had previously cut other women on the chest with a knife, and she burned insects and caterpillars. "Light a match, burn them, watch them squirm, back legs first, middle legs, back, then head." She also burned the hair on a cat.
- Although not all her friends regarded her as a respectable, law-abiding citizen, many of them were surprised by her act of murder.

As is so often the case, she did not fit the profile in all respects, but she certainly showed many of the features described.

CHILD KILLERS

Killers of children include their parents and others who are re-
sponsible for their care; pedophiles (see Chapter 8); as well as mass
murderers and serial murderers who kill indiscriminately. This section focuses on those who batter children. The nature of injuries to
a child arouses suspicion, such as the presence of new and old
bruises, as well as bruises on the backs of the legs—pre-schoolers
who fall usually have bruises on the front of the legs. Bruises on
both sides of the face are unlikely to be caused by falls. The child
who is gagged as punishment or to stop persistent crying has characteristic bruises at the corners of his mouth.

The child who steps in a bathtub of very hot water will have
burns on his feet and splash marks on his legs, the child who is
placed in very hot water will have burns over his entire buttocks
and legs. The infant who is held by his wrists and ankles then
dunked in scalding water will have burns shaped like a donut on
his buttocks. Cigarette burns are not usually accidental burns. Flexible objects used in beatings curl around the body. Ropes tied around
the wrists or ankles cause flesh blisters or pigmented chronic rope
burns. Wasted buttocks and a distended abdomen point to malnut-
rition or frank starvation. X-rays of bones, so necessary in suspected
deaths from child abuse, may show fractures in different stages of
healing.

Profile of Abusive Parents

- Immature, easily frustrated, poor impulse control.
- Expect their children to behave like much older children, set
  unusually high standards of behavior.
- Role reversal—expect children to take care of the parent's phys-
  ical, emotional, and sometimes sexual needs.
- Self-righteous—feel their policy of spare the rod and spoil the
  child is in the best interest of the child, some are very religious.
- May themselves have been victims of child abuse.
- Physical abuse provoked by child wetting pants or bed, soiling,

crying, lying, demanding attention or doing something wrong.
- Delay seeking medical care for injured child.
- Bathe and dress child before taking to the hospital.
- Take child to a different doctor or hospital each time medical care is needed.
- Show no concern or excessive concern.
- Explanation of the injuries may not match the child's story or may be inconsistent with the nature and extent of the injuries.
- Only one child may be battered, that child may be rebellious, sickly, illegitimate, a hindrance or a stepchild.
- Verbal abuse (bastard, slut, whore, etc.) accompanies physical abuse.
- Parents may come from any social class.
- Some parents are drug abusers or alcoholics.

In cases of fatal injuries, the first task is often to interview both parents to find out who is the likely suspect. Of course it may be the babysitter. The one who is evasive, repeats questions or changes the story to fit new evidence provided by the detective will be questioned more intensively. If the detective shows some awareness of the frustrations in looking after children, he is more likely to obtain a confession. "I've got kids of my own, I can relate to what you're going through. They push you and push you to the point you can't help what you're doing and you pop them. You just break; you lose control." A little empathy goes a long way. "This kid is driving you crazy, she deserves correction. Nobody intentionally harms a child, they're too precious, but I can understand the pressure that you were under."

Avoid terms like whipping and beating. Instead talk of discipline and correction—"You reacted" not "You beat the child." Deal with why it happened. The detective who becomes very angry at the thought of a parent, boyfriend or girlfriend of a parent, or a babysitter physically abusing a child is not likely to obtain a confession. He should remember that many of those who batter children were themselves battered by their parents. This does not excuse their behavior, but at least it becomes easier to understand it.

CHILDREN AND ADOLESCENTS
WHO KILL THEIR PARENTS

Children and adolescents who kill their parents tend to belong to one of three groups. Members of all three groups may have been physically or sexually abused by their parents and may conceal this information.

Antisocial or delinquent youths may also kill strangers. If the youth is a member of a juvenile gang, he may kill a member of a rival gang in a street fight, in revenge for loss of face or to gain status within the gang.

Unusually well-behaved youths with no prior antisocial or delinquent behavior may kill father to protect mother or sibling from assault by father. They may also kill a sexually seductive mother.

Children or adolescents with schizophrenia or organic brain disease may kill their parents.

Profile of Antisocial Youths Who Kill

- Broken home or poor home life.
- Parental physical or sexual abuse.
- Poor grades at school.
- Poor school attendance, suspension from school.
- No sports involvement.
- Persistent lying.
- Rebellious behavior.
- Alcohol and drug abuse.
- Impulsive, unreliable.
- Arrests for shoplifting, vandalism, theft, burglary, assault and juvenile prostitution.
- Membership in street gang or punk rock group with interest in heavy-metal music and satanism.
- Poor self-image, self-centered, few friends outside the gang.

Profile of Previously Well-Behaved Youths Who Kill Their Parents

- Broken home or poor home life.
- Parental physical or sexual abuse.
- Good grades at school.
- Good school attendance.
- Sports involvement.
- Works regularly in part-time jobs.
- Shows respect for authority.
- No alcohol or drug abuse.
- Reliable, anticipates needs of adults.
- No prior arrests or antisocial behavior.
- Deceptive appearance of maturity.
- Lack of empathy for others, arrogant, difficulty in forming close relationships.

ASSAULT

If men have nothing else to fight over they will fight over words, fancies, or women, or they will fight because they dislike each other's looks, or because they have met walking in opposite directions.

George Santayana, *The Life of Reason*

Whether the charge will be assault or murder may depend more upon the quick arrival of experienced paramedics and the presence of a skilled surgical team at the local hospital, than upon the motives and intentions of the assailant. In many assaults there is a mutual combat, and you don't have victims, you have losers. The guy who loses complains to the police.

Several studies of homicide and assault have shown more similarities than differences. Both crimes tend to occur in the same areas of a city, at the same times (especially on Saturday evening and early Sunday morning), and with the same distributions in age and sex among offenders and victims. The crimes are similar, and so are the methods of interrogation, but the stakes are greater for both the suspect and the detective in the crime of murder.

Chapter 7
ARMED ROBBERY KIDNAPPING AND HOSTAGE NEGOTIATIONS

A robbery is a perfectly rational transaction which includes the assumption that violence will be exercised if compliance to the robber's will is not forthcoming.

J.P. Conrad, *The Nature and Treatment of the Violent Offender*

An experienced robbery detective said that if a suspect is willing to talk about his family, he will be willing to talk about his robberies. He was making the point that you can't walk in and start questioning the suspect about his crimes. You've got to prime the pump. Do not lead him. Get what he has to offer first, as he may tell you something you do not know. If he has committed 20 to 30 armed robberies, he may have difficulty recalling all the details, especially if he has been using drugs. Ask him what was the first robbery he committed. He will always remember the first one.

If it was a fast food outlet, ask the suspect how many employees were there, were they male or female, how many customers and how much money did he get. Get him to tell you things that only a person who was present would know. Let him do that with each robbery that he remembers. Then ask him about each robbery in which he is a suspect, either because of the victim's description of the robber or because of the similarity in the way the crimes were committed.

Ask him about his method of robbing stores. This might include questions on planning. Perhaps he had a street map listing the locations of convenience stores or supermarkets belonging to one chain. What were his reasons for picking one store over another? Did he prefer stores with display-windows obscured by advertisements so that patrolmen driving by cannot see inside? Did he check for police patrols? Did he have an employee informant who was providing information? Did he case the store? Did he wait until there were no customers in the store?

Ask him about his choice of time for the stick-up, his use of a ski or stocking mask, false mustache, another shirt underneath or a change of clothing nearby. What type of firearm or other weapon was he using, or did he simulate a weapon? Was the gun loaded? Had he fired the weapon before the stick-up? What words did he use, or did he use a note? Did he purchase an item in order to get the clerk to open the cash register? (Robbers tend to purchase the same item, perhaps a pack of Camel cigarettes, in every robbery.) Did he jump over the counter or go behind the counter? Did he check under the cash register tray, or did he open the safe? What did he take?

Did the suspect taunt the victim, threaten to kill him or ask him to tell the police that he belonged to another ethnic group? Did he tie up, injure or sexually assault the victim? What items were taken? Did he have a getaway car, was it stolen, were the license plates altered or obscured? Was there another car parked a short distance away? Did he have a partner, and what was his role? Was he under the influence of drugs or alcohol?

If he is willing to write a statement, keep it brief. The longer the statement, the greater the likelihood of problems in court. For example, he may get one robbery confused with another. The suspect who refuses to say anything may confess when confronted with evidence against him, such as surveillance camera photographs of him committing the robbery, his fingerprints on the cash register or the written statement of an accomplice.

The driver of the getaway car may admit to driving the robber to the store, but claim that he had no idea that his passenger was going to commit a robbery. However, on questioning he may admit that he parked his car in a poorly lighted area behind the building instead of in front of the store. How did he know that his passenger robbed the store? Did he come back with money in one hand and a gun in the other hand? When the suspected armed robber is shown the videotaped statement of the driver he may become enraged, and tell the detective that the driver knew he was going to rob the store, and that he received some of the money.

When the suspect insists that he obtained only $75, and not $300, in a robbery, it may be that the victim inflated his loss, either because he wants to claim more from his insurance company, or because he took additional money himself from the store where he was employed. He may be willing to give a revised estimate of the amount taken. Otherwise there is the risk that the victim may not identify the robber in a line-up because he fears that his dishonesty will be exposed in court.

FALSE REPORTS OF ARMED ROBBERY

Almost 7 percent of all reports of armed robbery in Denver one year were found on investigation to be false reports. The detective who suspects a false report will question the victim at length and possibly request a polygraph test.

Profiles of False Reports of Armed Robbery

- Delay in reporting the offense.
- Location of the offense is notorious for drug sales, prostitution or homosexual activity. A robbery may have occurred, but not under the circumstances described by the victim. Inability to give the location is most often encountered in false reports. A

robbery in areas where robbery is almost unknown may be a false report.

- Description of the suspect. In false reports there is: (1) An exceptionally detailed description. For example, a bank teller who handed an accomplice $9,000, then tripped the bank alarm, and claimed that she had been robbed by a man who threatened to set off a bomb, gave a long description of his appearance, including "a light mark on his fourth finger as if he had removed a wedding ring." (2) A very poor description with no mention of race, height, weight or body build. (3) A description of a man who looks like a real villain indeed. (4) Or the victim describes himself.
- The victim gives a false or non-existent home address.
- The victim has a criminal record.
- Description of the offense. Includes improbable events, suspect has two guns; youthful victim sees the getaway car but has no idea of the make or model of the car; contradictory statements, a red and white coat becomes a black and white coat, a revolver becomes an automatic pistol. The account may suggest that the victim wants attention or sympathy.
- Amount of loss is much greater than might be expected, for example the loss of $2,000 is much greater than a day's business at a small tavern. If the money is from a paycheck, the victim may have spent it on a prostitute, gambling or liquor and does not want to tell his wife. The victim may need an excuse for his failure to pay his rent or his mortgage payment.
- Knife or gunshot wounds occur almost twice as often in false reports as in genuine robberies. The gunshot wound may have occurred in a suicide attempt, a family altercation, while playing with a gun or in a genuine armed robbery in which the offender was shot but was able to leave the scene. The offender then claims that he was shot by an armed robber.
- Loss of consciousness is reported 50 times more often in false reports than in genuine robberies. Loss of consciousness for several hours may be reported, yet there is no sign or slight evidence of head injury.

- Other offenses, in addition to robbery, also raise doubt. For example kidnapping, but victim does not take first opportunity to escape and delays calling police. Auto theft is reported in order to cover a hit-and-run accident that was not reported to the police. Prior false reports of robbery or burglary.
- Reluctance or failure of victim to come to the detective bureau for an interview.
- The account of the robbery given to the detective differs from the account provided to the patrol officer who took the robbery report.

KIDNAPPING

Whenever a kidnapping suspect is arrested and the location of the victim is not known, the victim's survival may depend on quick, skillful interrogation. For example, a victim who has been tied up and hidden in some remote location known only to the kidnapper, may die from lack of food or water. Miranda warnings are not needed when life is at stake, according to W.T. Pizzi's article in the *Journal of Criminal Law and Criminology*, 1985.

Kidnappers include:

- Sex offenders, who kidnap women or children on the street and take them to a safe location for rape and sometimes for murder (see Chapters 6 and 8).
- Armed robbers, trapped at the scene of the crime and criminals in custody kidnap citizens and use them as hostages in their efforts to escape.
- Men who seize children or adults for ransom. Some of these kidnappers are first offenders who start their criminal careers at the top; others are antisocial personalities. (see Chapter 4).
- Parents involved in child custody disputes, who kidnap their children, and then disappear from sight. They may hire private detectives to snatch the child. When the children are placed in school at some distant location, they may be told to lie about their names and previous addresses. The children may also lie

when questioned by the police, because they either love or fear the parent who has kidnapped them.

- Parents who hire so-called deprogrammers to kidnap sons or daughters (ages 16 to 25) who have joined cults. The deprogrammers, after kidnapping a cult member, try to persuade him or her to give up new religious beliefs and may also try to convert him or her to previously held beliefs.
- Jilted lovers who kidnap the former lover or friend in the hope of forcing a reconciliation. Previously the jilted lover may have harassed the former lover through obscene or threatening anonymous telephone calls, burglary, theft and vandalism.
- Terrorists, who kidnap people to obtain money, publicity or political concessions, such as the release of other terrorists from prison. Profiles vary from one terrorist group to another, but those directly involved in acts of terrorism tend to be socially isolated young men and women from 16 to 35 years of age, dissatisfied with their lot in life. (See profiles of terrorists, Chapter 11.)
- Women who kidnap newborn infants from hospitals, or kidnap older children, then claim them as their own children.

Profiles of Female Child Stealers

Manipulative Offender
- Age 18 to 40.
- Motive: to prevent desertion by husband or boyfriend or to win back his affection by claiming pregnancy and later birth of child.
- May have suffered recent miscarriage, or may be unable to have a child.
- Preoccupied with thoughts of pregnancy and having a child.
- May wear maternity clothes and padding to simulate pregnancy.
- May attend prenatal clinic or Lamaze sessions.
- May purchase baby clothes or obtain them as gifts from friends, possibly at "baby shower."
- Steals baby from maternity ward, may pose as nurse.

- Hysterical or immature personality.

Deprived Offender
- Age 18 to 35.
- Motive: wants to comfort herself by playing with or mothering a young child.
- Preoccupied with thoughts of pregnancy and having a child.
- May wear maternity clothes and padding to simulate pregnancy.
- May purchase baby clothes or obtain them as gifts from friends, possibly at "baby shower."
- Steals baby from maternity ward, or steals older child (a few months to eight or nine years of age) that she knows, perhaps from babysitting the child. On arrest she will claim mother was neglecting the child.
- Possible prior arrest for same offense.
- Childish, immature personality or hysterical personality. Some of these offenders are mentally retarded, many were themselves unwanted or neglected children.

Psychotic offender
- Age 35 to 55.
- Motive: to replace children taken from her because of her chronic mental illness or act based on delusional beliefs.
- Usually steals three- or four-month-old child from stroller while mother is shopping.
- Impulsive crime not preceded by wearing maternity clothing.
- Bizarre behavior, may be hallucinating and have delusional ideas.
- Rarely may kill the child.
- Usually suffers from chronic schizophrenia, but may have acute psychotic illness.

HOSTAGE NEGOTIATIONS

A waiting game is a winning game.

Instructors assigned to the Special Operations and Research Unit at the FBI Academy teach approximately 25 hostage negotiation schools a year for police officers. These instructors include special agents Frederick J. Lanceley, G. Dwayne Fuselier and Clinton R. Van Zandt. Their role is not simply academic. They have themselves served as hostage negotiators and as consultants to police officers during hostage negotiation incidents. Many of the negotiating techniques described below are based on their instruction, but this section does not represent the viewpoint of the FBI and no such claim is made.

THE HOSTAGES

A hostage is a person held as security for the fulfillment of certain demands. If a person has been seized by an offender and there are no demands, the offender may have homicide in mind, or homicide and suicide. When the victim seized is the offender's wife, some authorities would describe the seizure as a domestic dispute and not a hostage situation because there are no demands. Yet often there is a demand, "Go away, leave me alone." Even if the person says "It's too late," successful negotiation may still be possible.

THE HOSTAGE TAKERS

- Criminals trapped at the scene of their crime. For example, armed robbers in a bank.
- Prisoners in jails and penitentiaries in an attempt to escape, or to protest conditions in prison.
- A person with a grievance. For example, a man who believes he has been cheated by an investment company.
- Political terrorists.
- The depressed person who threatens the life of his hostage or kills the hostage in order to provoke the police to kill him, termed "suicide by cop."
- Psychotic people who may be acting in response to delusional beliefs.

THE NEGOTIATORS

Negotiators don't command, Commanders don't negotiate.

The negotiator should be a law enforcement officer, but for several reasons he should not be the chief of police. He may be called away to make other command decisions, he cannot stall for time by telling the hostage taker that he has to get the approval of a senior officer before agreeing to some demand, and he cannot blame police commanders for delays. Whenever possible there should be at least two negotiators so the second can monitor negotiations and provide advice.

Many good interrogators also are good hostage negotiators. The successful negotiator talks easily with people, is flexible and is a good listener. He is able to tolerate sustained stress without becoming irritable or short-tempered, and is capable of coping with impatient superior officers as well as impatient hostage takers. In short, he has to have the patience of Job and the persuasive powers of a gifted diplomat.

Some negotiators are too tough, others are too gentle. As M.S. Miron and A.P. Goldstein point out in *Hostage*, the aggressive, unyielding negotiator will needlessly threaten the lives of hostages. On the other hand, the negotiator who is too concerned with the feelings of the hostage taker, too concerned with being accepted and well-liked and too willing to yield to the hostage taker's demands, will fail to bring the negotiations to a satisfactory conclusion.

Family Members and Friends

As a rule, family members and friends of the family should not be used as negotiators. After a man had seized his wife and threatened to kill her, a friend of the family told police, "I know I can get them out, please put me on the phone. Please." He did not mention that he was having an affair with the man's wife. As soon as the husband heard this man's voice on the telephone, he shot and killed his wife and then killed himself.

Dwayne Fuselier points out that family members will say, "Let me talk to him, he'll listen to me." When they get on the phone, some will call the subject a jerk or tell him he's just screwing up again. Another will say, "Hang in there, Joey, we're all proud of you." Harvey Schlossberg notes that a man's family is a part of his problem and, as such, can make matters worse. He points to two cases in which a criminal asked that his wife be brought to the scene, yet in each case, when she appeared, the man shot his hostage then turned his gun on himself.

Sometimes a family member can be helpful. A negotiator, after talking to the parents and adolescent brother of a barricaded person who had shot two police officers, realized that the brother had a good relationship with the subject, and did not want him to die in a gun battle with the police. The brother told the subject, on the telephone, that there was no point in a permanent solution to a temporary problem. A short time later the subject surrendered.

THE NEGOTIATION

The negotiators should be in a room by themselves, with an officer outside the door to prevent the entrance of unauthorized people. One negotiator talks to the hostage taker on the telephone, while the other keeps notes and prints in block letters brief statements on what is happening, critical demands by the subject, deadlines and what is going wrong. These statements, penned on a "situation board," provide a summary of the situation and are especially valuable for relief negotiators when they come on duty.

On a blackboard there are diagrams of the area and of the building where the subject and hostage are located. A voice-activated tape recorder is used to record all conversation with the subject. Some police departments have large, specially equipped vans or motor homes with a soundproof room for the negotiators, a command post with telephone equipment, a toilet and food.

A list should be kept of all concessions granted to the subject. This list will prove valuable when he says "You haven't done anything for me" or when he asks "What have you done for me?" Lists should also be kept of the times of threats or talk of violence, the times hostages have been released and the times deadlines have passed without incident. These lists will prove useful when the scene commander wants an immediate report on how things are going.

Soskis and Van Zandt in a 1986 article in the journal *Behavioral Sciences and the Law* have listed indicators of the progress of the negotiation. "Positive negotiation progress is indicated by: (1) less violent content in the subject's conversations with negotiator; (2) the subject talking more to the negotiator; (3) the subject talking at a lower rate, pitch or volume; (4) an increased willingness on the part of the subject to talk about personal issues; (5) the release of hostages; (6) the negotiation getting past a deadline set by the subject without incident; (7) no one having been killed or injured since negotiations began or (8) a decrease in the number of threats made by the subject over the course of the negotiations." Negative indicators are the opposite of the indicators listed above. Soskis and Van Zandt also include reports that the subject has recently killed a significant other in his life, especially a child; a history of violence; refusal to negotiate, setting a deadline for his own death; and demands that officers kill him.

Establishing Communication

Face-to-face encounters can be fatal and are not advised. More than 20 negotiators, including experienced police officers, have been killed or wounded. Why risk your life? A note can be pushed under a door, but leave one corner in view to see whether it is taken inside. The use of a bull horn has obvious disadvantages including the fact that the hostage taker has to yell in reply. He may not respond because he thinks that he can escape or he hopes that the police will leave the area if he remains silent. He may be fearful of revealing his location to the police SWAT unit. Deaf people, non-English speaking, severely wounded, alcoholic, drug intoxicated or psychotic subjects may not speak to the negotiator.

The first task of the negotiator is to seize the telephone line to the suspect. This task may take the telephone company some time, especially when it is a line through a switchboard. Negotiations have been delayed because journalists are on the line to the hostage taker before the negotiators are in position. The telephone company can provide a new telephone number that only the negotiators know and can prevent the hostage taker from calling anyone other than the negotiator.

Fuselier stresses the need to isolate the subject so he can only communicate with the negotiator. If he gets on the phone to the media, to friends or to relatives, things can go downhill quickly. If the subject does not have access to a telephone, one will have to be provided for him, either an army field phone or other portable phone.

Establishing Rapport

Open with a positive statement. "My name is John Smith. I am with the Denver Police Department. I would like to help; who am I talking to? Would you tell me what is going on? I would like to hear your side, I know we can work it out." If there are several hostage takers, it is better to talk to the leader. He will make the decisions.

The usual techniques are used to form a bond with the subject. Listen for statements that show strong feelings and hook on to these feelings. "It sounds like you're really upset about that." Label the emotions. "You seem angry about that." Encourage him to talk about his feelings and his problems with occasional "Aha," "Yes," "Oh" and similar responses.

The negotiator talks slowly in a soft voice, especially when an agitated hostage taker is shouting threats and demands. Do not tell the subject to calm down. The negotiator's soft, slow voice has a calming effect. He tries to establish a climate of compromise in which civilized people try to reach agreement without resorting to violence.

Another ploy to calm a subject is to distract his attention. Among the methods suggested by Miron and Goldstein are asking a question or bringing up a topic, that is irrelevant to the hostage situation or giving a suggestion that indicates the subject can continue doing something he expects you to want him to stop or otherwise behave in a manner contrary to his expectations about negotiators or the police.

Repeat or paraphrase his statements, to show that you are listening to him and to keep the discussion going. Reflect his demands but soften them. If he demands a 747 jet plane and $500,000, reply, "You want a plane and money." Show attention, build self-esteem, listen sympathetically to his complaints, and do not show a judgmental, critical attitude. Minimize the significance of what he has done. It is most important to gain rapport before asking him about his weapons and the people with him.

Once rapport is established say to him "Bob, nothing much has happened, I think it would be best for you to put the gun down and come out." Plans should be made early in the negotiation with the tactical unit so that the subject can be told exactly what to do, if he should make a quick decision to come out. In talking to him do not use the word surrender. Other words that may reduce rapport include: kill, shoot, SWAT, judge, sentence and penitentiary. Also avoid stilted police jargon, such as complainant and perpetrator.

The friendly approach should not be overdone. One hostage taker later said, "The police officer was so nice to me I didn't trust him." Negotiators with a quick, natural sense of humor can use this talent to advantage.

The Importance of Time

As time passes the suspect's initial excitement and tension begin to diminish. It is important therefore, to slow everything down. Time permits the police to obtain more information on the hostage taker's personality, family and personal background, medical and psychiatric records, army record, criminal record, his weapons, terrorist affiliations and so on. Information can also be obtained on the hostages and the layout of the building where they are being held.

Time permits the negotiators to obtain similar information directly from the subject or his hostages. Time provides negotiators the opportunity to think through the best strategy for securing the safe release of the hostages. The tactical team can make better preparation for possible assault. The hostages may seize an opportunity to escape. Time also facilitates development of the Stockholm syndrome, which may be to the advantage of the hostages.

Demands and Deadlines

Avoid immediate, outright rejection of any demands, no matter how unreasonable they may be. This is to avoid provoking the hostage taker when he is in an angry, volatile state of mind. It is also part of the strategy of stalling for time.

If there are several demands, time can be spent in prolonged discussion of minor issues. The negotiator can summarize the demands, restate them, rephrase them, discuss them, review both sides of the issue and otherwise take up time, in much the same manner that bureaucratic committees take forever to reach decisions.

Meet reasonable demands, but not all at once in order to prolong the negotiations. Unless a concession is made to improve rapport, insist on something in return. "I'm doing this for you, will you do this for me?" for example; "I will arrange for food to be placed in such and such position; will you arrange for it to be picked up?" The person who takes the food to an agreed upon location may be able to take pictures surreptitiously. Establish routines for meals, don't give him more than what he requests and don't offer him anything.

The subject should be asked what food he wants. The number of sandwiches he requests may provide a clue to the number of people with him. Drugs, such as sedatives should not be placed in food or drinks. Do not set deadlines for yourself, such as "I'll have the coffee for you in 10 minutes." If the subject sets a deadine, "Get me a jet plane by 5 o'clock or I'll kill the hostages," bring up some other issue just before the deadline. For example, mention a prior request for cigarettes and discuss details of delivery while the deadline is passing.

If the subject starts fussing about a deadline, dream up some excuse for the delay, blame problems with the airline or police commanders, breakdowns in communication, and "Just give me a break; I'm having all kinds of problems; I'm doing the best I can." It is very rare for a hostage to be killed because a deadline has not been met.

There can be no substitution of hostages. Police officers should not volunteer to become a hostage in return for the release of a hostage. There is no glory in killing a civilian, but the subject gains status in his own mind by killing a police officer. Substitution of a hostage interferes with development of the Stockholm syndrome.

The subject may ask for a relative, his minister or some other named person in return for the release of all the hostages. But his intention may be to kill the substitute or to commit suicide in his presence, conveying the message, "It's your fault I'm dead." Always ask what he would like to talk to the person about. Avoid asking, "Why do you want that person?" because in general it is better to avoid asking "why" questions.

Weapons, drugs, alcohol and vehicles should not be provided. At a crucial stage of the negotiation, a vehicle may be promised to relax the hostage taker so that he is off-guard when a sudden assault is made. If the subject can be trapped as he walks to a car, it may be a tactical advantage to provide a car. Money can be provided if the subject is contained.

During the subject's recital of demands, the opportunity is taken to persuade him that he should come out. Use suggestion. It is "When you come out," not "If you come out" nor "Why don't you come out?" Constantly minimize his problems with the court, "You haven't done very much, you haven't injured anyone, we can work it out." Do not threaten the subject, but there must be a show of force by the police, even if the negotiator plays it down.

The Stockholm Syndrome

In 1973 a man armed with a submachine gun, plastic explosives and blasting caps held up one of Stockholm's largest banks and seized three women and one man as hostages. He demanded $700,000, firearms, bullet-proof jackets, a getaway car and the release from prison of a man serving time for armed robbery. The police arranged for this prisoner to join the bank robber, but did not respond to his other demands. In a phone call to the prime minister, one of the hostages said, "The robbers are protecting us from the police."

A police commissioner, who was allowed to look at the hostages, reported that they were sullen and showed hostility toward him. One woman practically curled her lip at him. They did not make any requests and he could detect no imploring looks. He noted a peculiar friendliness between the hostages and one of the robbers. Yet the robbers threatened to shoot the male hostage, placed nooses around the necks of all the hostages and told the police that any use of tear gas would lead to the strangling of the hostages as they fell unconscious.

Despite their ordeal during six days of captivity, the female hostages kissed their captors and the man shook hands with them upon their surrender to the police. Later in talking of their experience the hostages persisted in thinking of the police as the enemy, preferring to believe it was the criminals to whom they owed their lives. One female hostage found that she was identifying herself with the criminals, and on one occasion after her release, remarked to her doctor, "That was the morning we shot at the police."

In the Stockholm syndrome:
- The hostage develops positive feelings toward the hostage taker.
- The hostage develops negative feelings toward the police or FBI.
- The hostage taker develops positive feelings toward the hostage.

Whether the syndrome appears depends on time and the nature

of the relationship between the hostage taker and his hostage. Some hostages make clear their contempt for the hostage takers, and they are more likely to die if the subjects decide to shoot one of the hostages. Other hostages arouse negative feelings in the hostage takers, by complaining a lot or by showing cowardice. In short the hostages most likely to be shot are the macho guys who stare defiantly at the hostage takers and the wimps who groan.

A relationship is unlikely to develop when the hostage takers place sacks over the heads of the hostages and do not allow them to say anything. If, however, the hostage takers discuss with the hostages their grievances (whether toward an employer, the prison warden, an unfaithful spouse or the government), their financial problems, or their unhappy lot in life, then the two groups may begin to see each other in a different light.

The hostages begin to sympathize with the grievances of the hostage takers, despite their threats to kill them. They become angry at the police for their failure to meet the demands of the subjects for money, a getaway car or whatever. "Aren't our lives worth more then $500,000?" All this leads to a sense of camaraderie. The hostage takers learn something of the personal lives of their prisoners. The criminal who likes his hostage is less likely to kill him.

You might think that after their release, the hostages would feel angry at the criminals who threatened their lives, but this is not always so. Perhaps Machiavelli was right, "Men when they receive good from whence they expect evil, feel the more indebted to their benefactor."

Police can foster development of this syndrome by prolonging the negotiation, by instructing the hostages to talk to their captors whenever it is safe to do so, and to avoid provoking them; by providing food in bulk form, in the hope that subjects and hostages will work together preparing the sandwiches or hamburgers; and by asking the subjects the names of the people with them (avoid using the term hostage) and whether any are sick or in need of medical treatment. In any discussions with the subjects always refer to hostages by their first names. The purpose is to get the hostage takers interested in them as people.

The Suicidal Hostage Taker

Quick recognition of the suicidal subject is vital. He wants the police to kill him and is willing to kill a hostage to achieve his goal. Here are some clues provided by Van Zandt:

- His only demand is that you kill him.
- He refuses to negotiate.
- He sets a deadline for his own death.
- He demands a weapon, when apparently he has a weapon.
- He has just killed a "significant other" in his life, for example a spouse, parent or especially a young child.
- He has given things away, especially items of sentimental value.
- He provides you with an oral will, such as "I want my brother to look after my dog," or "I want my sister to have my watch."
- He has an elaborate plan for his death.

The Inadequate Personality

This man is a loser, an ineffective person who seems unable to cope with life's social and emotional demands. He is a failure at school and drops out before graduation. He is a failure at work and goes from one low-paying job to another. He is a failure in his married life and is probably separated or divorced from his wife. Unfortunately he may attempt to obtain the attention, wealth and power that he desires through some spectacular crime such as a skyjacking. He may be calm and polite, but often he starts off by shouting and screaming at those around him.

His demands for money in return for the release of hostages are often very high. He wants $1 million or possibly $30 million and a plane to Libya—right now. These exorbitant demands are a clue to the personality type of the hostage taker. His hostages recognize his weak personality and often feel sorry for him. The quick appearance of the Stockholm syndrome is another clue that the offender has an inadequate personality.

The initial approach of the negotiator is friendly and uncritical. "Joe, I understand your position, you've worked hard on this, you've been treated unfairly, you deserve a break, I can see where you're coming from." Every effort is made to boost his ego so that he feels that he is a very important person. Constantly reassure and compliment him. Give him the impression that he is making decisions. He may respond to a female negotiator. Once rapport is established, there is a gradual shift to a more directive approach. "Listen Joe, we've been here five hours, let's stop this, put your gun down, come on out."

Try to keep the media away as their presence at the scene may encourage him to prolong the event. Family and friends should also be kept out of sight, as he will see surrender in their presence as another in a long list of failures. Always try to prevent loss of face.

The Antisocial Personality

The antisocial personality may demand a lot of money, perhaps $500,000, but his demands are usually a lot more reasonable than those of the inadequate personality. There is a good chance that he has a criminal record that points to his chronic antisocial behavior. Prompt gathering of information on his background should provide the negotiator with the diagnosis. This is important as these people are streetwise and quick to pick up any mistakes by the negotiator.

As in any negotiation the initial approach is designed to establish rapport. You may point out how bright he is, but do not overdo it. Subtle praise is the order of the day, otherwise you will upset him. He likes to be involved in activities, so keep him busy on the telephone, then he will not pick on the hostages and dream up new demands. Do not criticize him for ill treatment of hostages, but compliment him for any favors he has shown them. Point out that such favors will be to his advantage.

Once rapport has been established, convince him that the release of hostages will be to his advantage. The tactics change. Now you begin to point out the reality that he will have to do time in prison, but you are quick to add: "You know how the system works, what's the chance of you're doing much time? You know all about plea bargaining, you know the prisons are overcrowded, and no one serves their full sentence, you get time off for good behavior, come out now, nobody has been seriously injured, we can tell the court that you cooperated."

The Paranoid Schizophrenic

Weird demands alert you to the possibility that you are negotiating with a psychotic paranoid schizophrenic. For the release of hostages he wants $10 or $100 million. He may tell you that he is carrying out a mission for God, or he may claim to be the Messiah himself. His demand may be for a bizarre message to be relayed on TV. He may tell you about his hallucinations and delusions, or you may obtain this information from the mental hospital where he has been treated.

Show an interest in his delusional beliefs, but do not argue with him about these beliefs. Do not try to prove to him that his delusions are false beliefs, out of touch with reality. You can say, "If I went through the things you told me about, I'd be pretty upset." Wait for him to say something that you can agree with. When he says, "I don't want to hurt anybody but . . ." respond "I know you don't want to hurt anybody, and it is good to hear you say that." If necessary, agree to the TV and news media publicizing his message. A psychiatrist or psychologist can provide advice.

The Depressed Hostage Taker

The extremely depressed person may speak slowly in a low tone of voice and it will take him a long time to answer questions. Unrealistic feelings of guilt for some minor transgressions in his life lead to feelings of hopelessness. He thinks that he is unworthy to live. His belief that his wife and family also face a bleak future may lead to his thinking that he would be doing them a favor by killing them before taking his own life. In these circumstances, murder followed by suicide is not rare. His hostages are usually members of his own family or someone close to him.

He is unlikely to initiate conversation and the negotiator may have difficulty talking to him. It is a good idea to ask him whether he has difficulty sleeping, does he wake up in the early hours of the morning? Is his appetite poor, has he lost weight and does he have difficulty in concentrating? The interviewer's sensitive inquiries may help him establish a bond with the depressed person. He may have the delusional belief that he is ruined financially, despite the fact that he is earning a salary ten times that of the negotiator and despite savings of many thousands of dollars. Do not argue with him, it is not wise to question delusional beliefs.

The majority of depressed hostage takers do not suffer from this severe form of psychotic depression. They may, however, also have both homicidal and suicidal tendencies and they are much more likely to have a criminal record. They are not likely to have the very slow speech and they will not have delusions, unless they are under the influence of hallucinogenic drugs.

Encourage any depressed person to talk about his problems, and discuss them with him. "Has anything happened in the last 24 hours that has upset you?" This question focuses on immediate problems that he may not have mentioned. Ask about heavy drinking, divorce or separation, job loss and financial difficulties. As one motive for suicide is revenge on someone, ask him if there is anyone he is angry at. Help him to recognize and express feelings of anger.

Especially if he is expressing ideas of hopelessness, "No one can help me," ask him whether he has thoughts of taking his own life. Has he taken any pills or done anything that might harm himself? If so, offer him immediate advice and help. Has he attempted suicide in the past? What method did he use? Has he had a problem with alcohol? Many suicidal people are alcoholics.

Women attempt suicide more often than men, but men more often commit suicide than women. The highest suicide rate occurs in depressed people over the age of 45. Suicide risk increases with age. Sudden disappearance of distress may not signal improvement, but calm once the decision is made to commit suicide.

Telling him that things aren't really that bad, is not likely to help him. Review possible solutions to his problems. Also focus on his interests, accomplishments and anything else likely to enhance his feelings of self-worth. Every effort should be made to restore his self-esteem. Show your concern for his welfare. Promise help in obtaining treatment.

Terrorists

Despite their repeated claims of readiness to die for their cause, many terrorists are willing to surrender, especially when great care is taken to enable them to do so without loss of face. In negotiating with them, tell them that they have made their point, their message has been reported on the evening news and will be repeated on the late news. Their demands have been heard and if they kill someone at this stage of the negotiations, the killing will discredit them in the eyes of the world. They should be told that they can surrender with dignity and honor.

Assist the Assault Team

If the decision is made to seize the hostage taker, the negotiator will keep him on the phone or persuade him to go to a location that suits the assault team. He may tell the subject not to be alarmed if he hears the sound of a generator, which has been brought in to provide emergency electrical power, when in fact it has been brought in to conceal noise made by the assault team. He may give the subject a false sense of success by promising that his demands will be approved shortly by the chief of police.

If a hostage is killed, the decision has to be made whether to launch an assault. While it is probable that if a captor kills one person, he or she may kill more, this is not absolute. The New York City Police Department hostage negotiation manual notes that on two occasions, a hostage was killed even after many deadlines had come and gone. Containment was maintained, negotiations continued and no assault was mounted. In time, the balance of the hostages were released unharmed and their captor was apprehended. An assault would surely have brought about casualties on all sides. Subsequent investigation indicated that the individual hostage who was killed had, in each case, engaged in conduct that appears to have precipitated or at least contributed to his demise.

Some commanders do not inform the negotiator when a decision has been made for the SWAT officers to make an assault. There is the fear that the negotiator will inadvertently betray the decision, through a change in his manner of speech or tone of voice. The British Special Air Service has a saying, "There should be no surprises for terrorists, except the last surprise."

THE BARRICADED SUBJECT

Hostage rescue incidents receive much more publicity than barricaded subject situations, but the latter are 10 times more frequent and can be just as dangerous for the police. When police officers intervene in a domestic dispute, to prevent a suicide or to arrest a suspect they may be faced with an armed subject who has no hostages but is unwilling to give himself up. He may tell the officers that he is armed and that he is not going to surrender, or he may fire on them without warning.

As in a hostage situation, the police at the scene will secure the area, and call in both negotiators and a SWAT unit or Special Reaction Team of highly trained, specially armed officers. The negotiators will attempt to establish communication and rapport with the barricaded subject, calm things down, stall for time, listen to what the subject has to say and generally proceed in much the same manner as in a hostage situation.

The person who is threatening suicide should be told that help can be provided at a local hospital emergency room. Extended discussion may show that the person is asking for attention and help rather than planning his own death. The criminal facing arrest will see the SWAT team as judge, jury and executioner. He may be depressed over the possibility of a long sentence and should be told, "You know the criminal justice system. How long do you think you're going to stay in prison, four or five years?"

Criminals are aware of the overcrowding in the prison system and the short memories of parole boards for crimes of violence that have not etched themselves on the minds of citizens. When they are threatening to kill themselves or police officers, they need to be reminded of the inefficiency of the criminal justice system. This may give them hope for the future. "Will you promise you won't kill me if I come out?"

John was asked to persuade a barricaded subject to give up a large hunting knife. The man, a prisoner in the security ward of a psychiatric hospital, had obtained the knife from a visitor. He attempted to bribe a guard to release him and when that failed he threatened the guard with the knife. He made many unreasonable demands that were not negotiable. After talking to him at length John was able to establish some rapport. He said that the judge had told his attorney he would get a 40- to 60-year sentence for the armed robbery of several convenience stores.

He felt he had nothing to live for and he was determined to escape as he could not face a return to the penitentiary. John pointed out that judges were no longer handing out such long sentences unless there was injury to a victim. There was a rather heated argument on this point but John was confident of his position. After further discussion the prisoner said he knew that John would call the police and that he would kill a cop before he was killed himself.

The police had already appeared at the hospital but were waiting outside the ward. John agreed that the prisoner might well succeed in his plan but it was not his intention to ask the police to subdue him. It was not fair to the police to expose them to such danger. Then John offered to permit the prisoner's wife to bring his baby to the ward. He had never seen the baby. After further discussion about the injustice of stabbing an unknown policeman, the prisoner handed over the knife. He received a 40- to 60-year sentence.

He escaped from the penitentiary, but was arrested after a man was killed during an armed robbery in a hotel. He was charged with murder, and later John was ordered to examine him by a federal judge. He did not bear John any ill will because he knew that John was speaking in good faith when he had told him, many years earlier, that there was no chance that he would get a 40- to 60-year sentence.

When all else fails, allow the family, the priest and others to try to persuade the barricaded subject to give himself up. There are no hostages whose lives may be placed in danger. If the subject later fires at the officers and dies the family cannot then say, "If only you had let us talk to him, we would have got him out alive."

Chapter 8
RAPE AND OTHER SEX OFFENSES

Unnatural deeds do breed unnatural problems.
Shakespeare, *Macbeth*

Men do not like to admit that they have obtained sex by force, so they either deny committing the crime, or they claim that the woman agreed to have sex. Victims of sexual assault often are reluctant to reveal the full extent of their humiliation by the rapist. Even so, the interviewer is more likely to obtain the cooperation of the victim than of the offender. It is important, therefore, to make sure that the victim is questioned in depth about the circumstances of the crime, keeping in mind the profiles of sex offenders.

Offender's initial approach
- Surprise attack—steps from concealment, hides in victim's car.
- Blitz attack—direct immediate physical assault.
- Con approach—needs directions, "Where is Vine Street?" Needs help, "Can you help me find my lost puppy?" Wants to use phone, pseudo police, pseudo authority, photography or modeling scam, repairman, offers to drive victim home from party or tavern.
- Burglary—method of entry, shuts off electrical power.

- Victim hitchhiking.

Control
- Threats—harm or death to victim, victim's family.
- Physical force—holding tightly, slapping, punching, sadistic.
- Weapon—knife, gun, simulated gun, tool such as screwdriver or hammer, glass, chemical such as Mace, acid or chloral hydrate. Weapon of choice or opportunity.
- Retraints—handcuffs, tie with rope or cloth, gag, blindfold, cover face.

Attitude
- Abusive, forceful statements, foul language, "If you scream, I'll kill you. I'm going to fuck you, bitch."
- Apologetic, seeks reassurance of sexual prowess, "I'm going to make love to you, I won't hurt you if you do what I say."
- Firm attitude.
- Change in attitude, what triggered change.

Sexual assault
- Offender removes victim's clothing, orders victim to undress, rips or cuts clothing. Offender clothed or naked.
- Vaginal, oral, anal intercourse, digital manipulation, inserts foreign object.
- Kiss or bite breast, genitals, anus.
- Offender masturbates self, makes victim masturbate him.
- Ejaculation, premature, retarded, on body, failure to ejaculate, semi-erection, impotence, repeated sex.
- Urination or defecation.
- Hit, cut, stab, burn or other injury.

Theft and destruction
- Items taken, damaged or destroyed such as money or clothes.
- Arson.

Before leaving
- Offender threatens to kill her or her family if she calls the police.

- Offender makes her douche and shower.
- Disables telephone.
- Locks victim up.

Alcohol and drugs
- Offender.
- Victim.

Victim resistance
- Runs, cries for help, persuasion, refuses to cooperate, fights.
- Offender response—restraint, threat, violence, negotiates for substitute activity such as oral instead of vaginal sex, or he leaves the scene.

Victim, additional questions
- Telephone surveys, obscene, threatening or hang-up telephone calls, notes or letters. Prior rapes.
- Feeling of being watched or followed, prowlers.
- Repairman or salesperson in home or apartment.
- Disagreements with fellow employees, neighbors or others.
- Theft or loss of identification.

Personality and lifestyle
Obtain from the victim her assessment of the personality and lifestyle of the rapist. Is he a wimp or is he macho, illiterate or well educated, with low or high self-esteem, and so on. The interviewer should also assess the victim's personality and lifestyle. Is she a loner, swinger, bisexual, lesbian, prostitute, alcoholic or drug abuser?

PROFILES OF RAPISTS

Lecturers from the Behavioral Science Unit of the FBI National Academy have described the power-assurance rapist, the power-assertive rapist, the anger-retaliatory rapist, the anger-excitation rapist and the opportunist rapist.

Power-Assurance Rapist
81 percent

The power assurance rapist accounts for four out of five arrests for rape or attempted rape. He has been called "The gentleman rapist" because he avoids profanity and apologizes for his behavior. He is usually a passive, inadequate person, a loner with few friends who has difficulty relating to women. An unmarried man, he resides with his parents or lives alone. A very domineering mother may account for his lack of self-confidence.

His job is menial and requires little or no contact with the public. He sees himself as a loser. He is not likely to be a car salesman. If he was in the armed services, he probably received a general discharge. He is not athletic, and he spends his leisure time in porno bookstores and movie theaters. His collection of pornography is hidden from sight. There may be a history of arrests for peeping, obscene telephone calls or burglary.

He selects victims, about his own age, give or take three years, who live near his home or place of employment. Usually he starts out raping women who live near his home. He watches potential victims and selects women who live alone or with small children. A favorite tactic is to tell the woman to cooperate or he will harm her children. He will break into her home between midnight and 5 a.m. Great care is taken to conceal his face from the victim. He wears a mask or covers her face and warns her not to look at him.

Usually his weapon is one of opportunity, such as a kitchen knife, that he picks up in the victim's house. He uses the minimum force necessary to maintain control, and he asks the victim to remove her own clothing. The sexual assault takes place in a short period of time and is not repeated. If there is any sexual dysfunction, it is usually premature ejaculation or impotency. He will do what the victim allows him to do. If resisted he will desist, leave, negotiate for some lesser sexual act, ("Well how about a blow job, a hand job?"), but he may threaten his victim in order to obtain her compliance.

Often he will ask for verbal reassurance regarding his sexual performance. "Am I better than your boyfriend? Tell me you like it; tell me you love it." He may question her about her work, her boyfriend and her social life. He wants to believe that the victim is enjoying the experience, and he may ask her for a date or telephone her the next day. He may have called her before the day of the rape. Before leaving he may apologize, but he will take a souvenir with him. Several days later he may telephone her and ask her for a date.

Rapes occur every seven to fifteen days, and as he gains more confidence he will move farther from his home in search of suitable victims. The first few rapes are clustered around his home. If he is a deliveryman, he may rape in the area where he makes deliveries. Usually he walks to and from the scene. The rapes stop only if he is sick or in jail. He will only kill if he is cornered and scared. A diary of his sexual assaults may be hidden in his room. If he is arrested, the interviewer should use counseling techniques with an empathic approach.

Power-Assertive Rapist
12 percent

This macho male has no need to reassure himself of his masculinity. He is athletically inclined and is very body conscious. A good dresser, he drives a flashy car or four-wheel-drive pickup, and he frequents singles bars. He uses, but does not abuse, alcohol or drugs because he likes to be in control of himself at all times. He may have been married several times, but his marriages do not last long because of his domineering, selfish attitude and his infidelity. He is very self-centered and cannot stand criticism.

A high school dropout because of disciplinary problems, he may have served in the armed services, probably in the Army or Marines, and his service may have been terminated administratively. Although he dislikes authority, he may seek employment as a police officer. He is likely to have a macho "hard hat" job. He may be a truck driver. If he has a criminal record, there will be arrests for crimes against property or for domestic disturbance. He is likely to be a "gun nut" and may collect Nazi memorabilia.

His purpose in rape is to express his virility. He is entitled to sex because he is a man. He is bolder, and will select victims away from where he works or lives. The rapes occur between 7 p.m. and 1 a.m., but usually in the early evening hours. The victim may be one of opportunity, someone he encounters whom he has not seen before. He may select a woman he has met in a bar, perhaps someone he has dated a few times. She will probably be within three years of his age.

If he has a weapon, it is one of his own choice. If resisted, he will hit, slap or threaten, and will not hesitate to rip his victim's clothing. He uses profanity and is very selfish in his actions—verbal, physical and sexual. He may start with a con approach, but if necessary will resort to direct physical assault. He does not wear a mask, but may try to hide his face by remaining in the dark and telling his victim not to look at him.

There may be repeated sexual assaults on the victim, including anal assault. If there is any sexual dysfunction, it will be retarded ejaculation, a problem that he also has with his wife or girlfriends. There is no attempt to contact the victim at a later date.

Anger-Retaliatory Rapist
5 percent

His purpose is to punish or degrade women. When he has suffered some injustice, whether real or perceived, at the hands of some woman, he gets even with all women by using sex as a weapon. It matters not to him that his victim may be a stranger. The rape is not carefully premeditated, but occurs on the spur of the moment. There is a blitz attack, which often occurs near his home, perhaps after a fight with his wife or an argument with his mother. He selects a victim about his own age or older. She may be someone he knows or has just met in a bar.

The attack is sudden, with any weapon at hand. He will strike her with his fists or a club, and he may kick her before ripping off her clothing. There is much profanity, and he may continue to beat her during the sexual assault. Anal sex precedes oral sex, and he may ejaculate in her face. Despite his brutality, this type of offender does not kill. The attack is brief and little time is spent with the victim. If there is any sexual dysfunction, it will be retarded ejaculation.

These offenders may come to the attention of the police because they are stopped for speeding after the fight at home or after the rape. The officer may remember that the speeder had blood on his hands. He may be arrested for fighting in a bar after the rape. A check of domestic violence reports may show that the wife made a complaint of assault by her husband on the night of the rape. She probably reported that he left the home angry and upset. It is important to check speeding, fighting and domestic violence reports on the night of the rape to see whether any of the suspects resemble the rape suspect.

Previous domestic disputes, possibly over his affairs with other women, may have resulted in court ordered mental health treatment because of his assaults on his wife. He probably married when he was very young. He is moody and argumentative, has a violent temper and may have been arrested for disorderly conduct. Alcohol abuse occurs, but he is a loner and does not drink in groups. An action-oriented person, he likes contact sports and works as a laborer or construction worker. He is a high school dropout. This offender will have any type of car. Although he will feel some guilt about the rape, within six months or a year he will rape again. Pornography is not a factor.

If the offender is arrested, the interviewer should use a very businesslike approach. It is a nonhostile approach, but the pressure on him is gradually increased. It may be helpful to start with a woman detective as a partner in the interview and then have her leave. These offenders account for about 5 percent of the arrests for rape.

Anger-Excitation Rapist

This is the most dangerous rapist. His purpose is to inflict pain, both physical and psychological. "Scream you bitch, scream." He seizes her a long way from his home or place of work. His rapes are carefully planned, and his initial approach is designed to enlist the cooperation of his victim. He seeks help, or directions, claims to be a police officer or otherwise persuades the victim to get into his car or come with him. Once the victim is under his control, he changes dramatically. He immobilizes his victim, he blindfolds, gags and handcuffs her, or otherwise places her under his complete control.

He has a weapon of his choice; indeed, he may have a rape kit consisting of gloves, mask, knife, blindfold, handcuffs or other restraints, Polaroid camera and tape recorder. He likes to have a record of the rape, which he can enjoy over and over again by playing the tapes or looking at the photographs. There is much sexual activity, little or none at all because sex is not his main concern. He may select victims who resemble each other. Usually he takes her to a place where he believes that he can assault her without risk of interruption.

His pattern of behavior may change as he learns quickly from experience. If he has a sexual dysfunction, it will be retarded ejaculation. He is likely to cut or tear off the victim's clothes, and his language will be commanding and degrading. Occasionally he may have an accomplice. In his home there may be S and M literature, Nazi paraphernalia, or detective magazines.

His IQ is above average, and he may have a college education. If he was in the armed services, he may have served as an officer. He is probably in his 30s, has a "good marriage" and a white-collar job, his car is clean and well maintained. Criminal investigation will involve inquiry for similar offenses in other jurisdictions, as well as review of check and credit card receipts. The approach on interrogation will depend on the information available on him. "Do you want your wife and kids to go through a trial" may be effective.

Opportunist Rapist

The burglar who robs a home or convenience store and finds a suitable victim for rape may take advantage of the situation if the victim does not appear likely to resist such an assault. The offender may be under the influence of alcohol or drugs. He is usually a youthful offender who does not repeat this offense.

Profile of Power-Assurance Rapist

- Rapes between midnight and 5AM, every 7 to 20 days.
- Selects victims by watching and window peeping.
- Seeks woman, about his age, living alone or with small children, and attacks her in her home.
- Weapon of opportunity, often knife.
- Covers victim's face or he wears ski mask to prevent identification. Asks her to remove clothing.
- If victim resists he leaves, negotiates for lesser sex act, threatens to harm victim or her children, or uses minimum force necessary to obtain compliance. Apologetic, little or no profanity. After several rapes, use of force may increase.
- Vaginal sex, possibly premature ejaculation or impotence.
- Asks victim to say she likes him and his sexual performance.
- Socially inadequate, loner, lives alone or with parents, menial job, frequents porno movies theaters and bookstores, arrests for peeping, burglary.
- No vehicle, first rapes within walking distance of his home.

Profile of Power-Assertive Rapist

- Rapes between 7 PM and 1 AM, every 20 to 25 days.
- Victim of opportunity, may meet in bar or date two or three times.
- Woman about his age, overpowering or "con" approach, domineers victim, rapes indoors or outdoors.
- Weapon of choice.
- No mask, may try to hide face, not let victim look at him.
- Slaps, hits, threatens, rips clothing, uses profanity.
- Repeated sex, anal then oral, vaginal, possible retarded ejaculation.
- Macho type, body conscious, athletic, frequents singles bars, hard hat job, truck driver, law enforcement officer.
- Married or divorced, arrests for domestic disturbance or crimes against property.
- Flashy vehicle, sports car or four-wheel-drive pickup.

Profile of Anger-Retaliatory Rapist

- Rapes any hour of day or night, irregular six-to 12-month intervals, after fight with wife or "put down" by woman.
- Victim of opportunity, in own neighborhood or near work.
- Woman same age or older, blitz attack.
- Weapon of opportunity, fists, feet, club, beats victim before, during and after sexual assault.
- Anal then oral sex, vaginal sex, possible retarded ejaculation.
- Much profanity and degrading language.
- May have been arrested for domestic disturbance, speeding or fighting on the night of the rape.
- Loner, drinker, trouble-maker, explosive temper, sports fan, laborer, construction worker, heavy equipment operator.
- Married man, abuses wife and children, arrests for fighting, family disputes, drinking.
- Any type of car.

Profile of Anger-Excitation Rapist
The Sadistic Rapist

- Rapes any hour of day or night, irregular intervals.
- Selects victims of similar appearance or something else in common, age varies.
- "Con" approach, then handcuffs, or ties with rope, takes victim to house or isolated area or rapes in van.
- Weapon of choice, revolver, pistol.
- Gloves, mask, included in rape kit.
- Rips clothing, degrading language, tortures, tape records, photographs, much or little sex, possible retarded ejaculation, may kill.
- May have accomplice, one dominates the other.
- In his 30s, good appearance, very neat, compulsive, high IQ, often college education, white-collar job, may travel a lot.
- Married, family man, no arrest record, no remorse.
- Vehicle well maintained, rapes far from home or work.

Profile of Opportunist Rapist

- Youthful offender.
- Possibly under influence of alcohol or drugs.
- Rape not planned.
- Occurs during robbery of a convenience store or burglary of a home.
- Likes appearance of victim.
- Victim, usually young, does not appear likely to resist.
- Victim is not physically injured.
- Rapes only once.
- Tends to leave evidence at the scene.

INCEST

A detective who was unusually successful in obtaining confessions from men suspected of incest, describes his philosophy and his approach:

"The first thing I do is shake his hand; most cops don't. I never put myself above him. First, I learn as much about him as possible, his values in life, what is important to him, the family he grew up in, his interest in his family and his job. We're talking about hours and hours of interviewing. The things that hurt him. The make-up of his family, his wife.

" 'Do you like your wife; how does she treat you, does she listen to you; does she understand you; does she bitch at you all the time; are your values important to her; is she a cold person or is she a loving person; how do you feel around her; is she a satisfactory sexual partner; are you satisfied physically, emotionally, spiritually; is there a bond between you or is it just sexual exercise?'

"In most incest cases there is a role reversal. The woman controls him sexually, turns him off, puts him down sexually. 'She's not giving you what you need, the closeness, the bonding between two human beings, the intimacy you want.' I reinforce his viewpoint. 'I don't understand why she'd treat you that way. You care for her obviously. You're really being put down by this woman. I don't understand why she'd treat you this way.'

"I talk to him about his relationship with his kids, what they mean to him. 'What do you do with your kids; do you eat meals with them; tell me about the good times; how important are the kids to you; what does your wife think about your relationship with them; do you think you are a good father?' I question him about each of his children. 'What do you do together with your son, play baseball, take him to the Bronco games?' I talk to him about the Broncos for about 15 minutes, showing a common interest.

"I question him in depth about his relationship with his daughter. 'How do you feel when you're around her; do you enjoy her company; how do you feel about her; why is she special to you; does she understand you, listen to what you say; is she affectionate; is she more or less affectionate than your other children; if you had a choice would you like your wife to be as affectionate and caring as this child?' Their eyes light up.

" 'Do you hug your kids, touch them, kiss them goodnight?' That's when incest occurs. Emphasize how cute or beautiful this girl is. She is really a doll. 'I can can see why you think she is really special. Does she sit on your lap; kiss you goodnight; hug you? Is she more affectionate than your wife?' I'll talk about the flirtatiousness of young girls, they can get daddy to do something daddy's boss couldn't get him to do. Young girls get their way with dad by being flirtatious. Both father and child receive some benefit. She gets positive reinforcement from dad, she's loved and cared for, and she gains control.

"I offer excuses. 'Your daughter is upset with you right now. She loves you, cares for you, and does not want to hurt you, but something's happened that's caused her to be afraid, frightened.' I'm not going to tip my whole hand as to what the girl has told me. 'Occasionally you brush your hand against her breast, I understand how something like that could happen accidentally or she may have misinterpreted something. For example, tucking your child into bed, you're going to touch her in some way. Obviously you didn't mean to hurt your daughter.

"'Maybe your daughter misinterpreted your goodnight kiss (in which he kissed her on the mouth and put his tongue in her mouth). Does she seem to want more affection; did she want you to stay and talk to her longer; did you sit on the edge of her bed or lay down alongside her to talk to her. I can understand your daughter is beautiful, gorgeous, so pretty, so cute, so pleasant. I can understand how your physical contact got a little out of hand. This is what I think happened. I don't think you went in the room with the idea of touching your daughter.'

"Do not use the words molest, fondle, or assault. Instead talk about touching or carressing. You might use the word fondle later on in the interview. 'I think your daughter was afraid, but she wanted to please you. She didn't understand what was going on.' Hang a guilt trip on him. 'She trusts you, she loves you; what you say she wants to believe.' Get him to admit she is flirtatious. 'Do you see her running around in her panties and bra? If you did see your 14-year-old daughter who is developing into a woman . . .' Get him to think of her as a woman, not as a child, even if she is only seven or eight years old.

" 'Your daughter should know better than to swing her butt in front of you. That's just asking for trouble. You're a normal man, normal men have sexual feelings. I can understand if there was a night your wife had been particularly tough on you, bitching at you, griping at you, putting you down and putting you down sexually, how you might have sexual feelings for your daughter. What do you do if your daughter shows she has sexual feelings, how do you handle that, you can't put her away, she's your daughter, you care about her?

'I don't think that what happened was meant to be sexual, I don't think that's what you intended, I think you intended to show your daughter you cared for her, I think you let your physical feelings take over. Sexual contact feels good. I really care what happens to you, to your family, to your kids.' When a man loosens up, he's going to talk to you. It's like pulling teeth to get an admission of incest. In incest cases you need an admission unless the man is caught in the act."

CHILD MOLESTERS

Child molesters include pedophiles who have a sexual preference for children. Many incest offenders are not simply men denied sex by their wives, but pedophiles who prefer children to adults as sexual partners. Research using a plethysmograph, which measures the volume of the penis, shows that many incest offenders are sexually aroused by pictures of young children. Sociopathic sex offenders assault both children and adults. They take advantage of any situation that offers them money or sex. Schizoid and inadequate personalities who feel unable to approach a woman for sex may pick on a non-threatening, vulnerable victim such as a mentally retarded child or a senile adult.

Profile of Pedophile Offender

- Usually single, has either not dated or dating has been limited. Lives alone or with his parents. May adopt or try to adopt a child.
- If married he has infrequent sexual intercourse with his wife, for example once every three months. On those occasions he may ask her to shave her pubic hair, ride a trike and dress like a young child with bobby socks and pigtails.
- Marriage is often to a woman who already has children. Divorce occurs when all her children are too old for his sexual taste.
- Occupation as teacher, school bus driver, camp counselor, photographer, pediatrician, priest, park and recreation director or similar job, little league coach or other volunteer work with children.
- Frequent, unexplained moves. He has to leave town suddenly because an angry father has threatened to file charges, notify his employer or beat him up. His employer, possibly a hospital or church, has told him to leave town after finding out about his activities with children.
- Premature separation from the military. The reasons may not be clear from reading official records, because there is insufficient evidence to charge him with child molesting.
- Hobby which brings him in touch with children; for example, he is a clown who performs in hospitals and for social groups or he is a photographer who likes to photograph children at rock concerts and beauty pageants.
- His home may include toys, games, stereos and rock posters. Some homes have been described as shrines to children or as miniature amusement parks (Lanning).
- Pornographic books pictures and videotapes, as well as a videocassette recorder and photographic equipment to record his perverse sexual acts.
- Member of NAMBLA, North-American Man/Boy Love Association; PIE, Pedophile Information Exchange; (PAN), Pedo-Alert Network; Rene Guyon Society or Lewis Carrol Collecter's Guild.

- Prior arrests for child molesting, impersonating a police officer, writing bad checks or violating child labor laws (Lanning).
- The pedophile may have been a victim of sexual or physical abuse in childhood.

Pedophiles usually seduce their victims. They seem to have an uncanny ability to select children who are likely to respond to their advances, and unlikely to complain to their parents or to the police. Thus, they may approach only one of a group of children, usually a child who is unloved or neglected by his parents. Often the children are from families in poor financial circumstances. There is usually an age and gender preference, for example boys from three to five, six to twelve or thirteen to fifteen years of age. Many pedophiles molest both boys and girls.

The seductive pedophile who bribes his victims does not resort to violence. If the child screams, he may suffocate or otherwise kill his victim, but violence was not intended at the outset. Sadistic pedophiles may kill some of their victims.

Interviewing techniques are similar to those described for the incest offender. The suspect should be treated with great respect. If the arresting officers have been scornful in their attitude and have not loosened tight handcuffs, the suspect will be very resentful, but may appreciate a different approach by the detective. Statements such as "It was an accident. I didn't mean to touch her vaginal area," and "She unzipped my pants and grabbed my penis and I became extremely angry," should not lead to immediate confrontation.

These offenders may see themselves as teachers of the children and not as sexual deviates. "You genuinely like kids and this just got out of hand." "I do this every day, and I know that kids aren't always innocent." You can say, "I can understand your position," but not "I agree with your actions," or "I would have done the same thing myself."

Confessions are important because they may save a child from having to appear in court. If the confession involves many offenses, the offender will realize the risk of a contested trial and a plea bargain or guilty plea reduces the risk of an appeal to a higher court.

INTERVIEWING CHILD VICTIMS

In many police departments, detectives investigating sexual offenses against children work closely with psychiatric social workers from the department of social services or a similar agency. In major investigations, a child psychiatrist may be called upon to interview the child. Qualified professional social workers and doctors can assist in the evaluation of the child's competency to testify, the credibility of his or her allegations, and the need for treatment. Especially in major cases involving very young children, every effort should be made to videotape the initial interviews.

Often a question is raised about the possible misuse of leading questions and suggestive comments. A videotape tells it all, and may save the child from repeated diagnostic interviews on the request of the defense attorney. D.P.H. Jones and R.D. Krugman have described the abduction, sexual abuse and attempted murder of a three-year-old girl. She was dropped through the toilet seat of a mountain outhouse into the fluid six or eight feet beneath. Three days later two birdwatchers found her, and she was flown by helicopter to a hospital.

When her rescuers asked her what she was doing inside the pit, she replied "I live here," and then cried for her mother. She survived because the cesspit was leaking and only contained one foot of sewage, and because she gathered sticks in the pit to make a platform to escape some of the fluid. Five days after her abduction, she picked a suspect from six photographs. At a preliminary hearing, testimony was presented that she was having frequent night terrors in which she would scream "get me out, get me out." The judge decided she was unavailable for testimony in court.

The psychiatrist's suggestion that her testimony could be provided under controlled conditions that protected her emotional well-being was accepted by the court. In a videotaped interview watched through a one-way glass screen, the psychiatrist had a microreceiver in one ear so that he could ask the child questions suggested by the district attorney and the defense attorney. She gave her account of the crime, but not in as much detail as in interviews closer to the time of the crime and was not upset by the interview.

Fifteen months after the abduction, the suspect confessed that he had sexually abused her in the exact manner she had described. Under a plea bargain agreement, he was sentenced to 10 years in prison. The case shows that a three-year-old child can accurately recall her abduction, sexual abuse and the attempt to kill her.

As in any interview, it is important not to talk down to the victim. The use of anatomical dolls facilitates the interview. If the victim shows that the suspect touched her on the genitals, ask her "I know what I would call it, what do you call it?" The terms used by children to describe their genitals vary according to their age, culture and upbringing. A boy might use the term "pee pee" or "ding dong"; a girl "taco" or "private parts." A very young girl may have difficulty distinguishing between vagina and anus. Pictures, for example of an erect penis, may also be useful.

The child may use one doll to talk to another doll. Ask who the dolls are rather than tell the child the identity of each doll. As some children use the term daddy to refer to more than one person, ask "Does that daddy have another name?" Let the child tell his or her own account of the molesting. After he or she has finished, ask questions such as "Did he take his clothes off? Did his penis (weiner) get big; did anything come out of it? Did you have any pain? (If yes,) did he put anything inside you? What? Where? (Keep in mind that to a very young child pressure on the genital area can feel like penetration.) Did anyone tell you not to tell; did anyone else touch you; did this happen to anyone else? Did anyone play games with you, tickle you in your private parts? Did anyone take pictures? Where was Mom when Dad was doing this? Show me in this doll house."

Avoid asking why questions, and do not use the expressions "hurt you" and "do bad things." It is usually easier for children to talk about a recent sexual assault by a stranger than about repeated sex activities over a long period with someone they know, especially if they like them. If a child feels that the interviewers can be trusted, he or she is more likely to speak up. A boy may want to draw a picture; and a girl may want to use her own dolls. Toward the end of the interview, check to see whether the child is resistant to suggestion, for example ask if two persons were involved when it is known that there was only one offender. Do not make promises to the child that you cannot keep.

False Accusations

In child custody suits or disputes over visitation rights, a parent may encourage a child to make false accusations of sexual assault against the other parent. The child comes to the interview and quickly makes a statement about the molesting. This occurs in every interview. D.P.H. Jones and J.M. McGraw list important cues--accounts that are delivered in response to the slightest of prompts from the interviewer, or related in a rehearsed, packaged manner with an absence of appropriate emotion, are considered with suspicion as are those that lack the usual reserve or hesitancy. Furthermore, in false reports the child provides little information about the molesting.

The genuine victim is embarrassed, and may be reluctant to go into details, but eventually gives specific information with great feeling, "It was yucky; the white stuff came out." In false reports there is a lack of detail. The child does not provide date, time, place and circumstances of each incident, because no plan was made to back up the accusations. Often the words used by a very young child, for example vagina, suggest coaching by an adult. There may be no threats or other coercion, and the account may be limited to a vague complaint of touching. Often there are inconsistencies. The assault takes place in the living room, yet on the next interview the teenager, without being aware of the discrepancy, says the assault took place in the bedroom.

Usually, children who make false reports are girls between 12 and 17 years old. Teen-agers who are angry at their parents or who want to escape parental discipline may make false reports to get back at their parents or to be removed from the home. The daughter who resents her stepfather may try to get him out of the home by claiming sexual assault. These teen-agers may have a history of

skipping classes at school, poor grades, arriving home late from
school, alcohol and drug abuse, shoplifting or other delinquent activities, and association with rebellious or antisocial adolescents.
There are teen-agers of good reputation who are influenced to make
false reports by the recent newspaper publicity on sexual assaults
within the home.

Chapter 9
BURGLARY, THEFT, CHECK AND CREDIT CARD OFFENSES

Every rascal is not a thief, but every thief is a rascal.

Aristotle

The more information the suspect thinks you have, the better the chance of getting a confession. The crime scene is a good source of information. In a burglary the detective should, whenever possible, review the crime scene with the victim. The crime scene does not always speak for itself. If a window is broken ask the victim whether the window was broken before the burglary. If the detective finds something thrown on the floor, he should not assume that the burglar threw it. He should ask the victim. It boggles the mind of the suspect if you tell him how he committed the crime.

You do not need this information in the written confession, but it is useful in questioning the suspect. If the detective has to ask the suspect how he got inside and what he did once he was inside, the suspect will key on that, and the chances of getting a confession are not good. Traditionally detectives ask who, what, when, where, why and so on, but in the crime of burglary the detective has to make some statements about the crime to show the burglar he knows what he is talking about.

Fifteen to 20 percent of burglary reports are inaccurate. The patrolman makes an error, or the victim adds to the value of items stolen. He claims that a rocking chair was damaged in the crime, but the detective notes that it is not fresh damage. The cash loss is often exaggerated. The detective should ask the victim how the figure was arrived at. This gives the victim the opportunity to scale down his loss. Was the stereo set really worth $2,000?

There is the usual background check of the suspect before the interview, and there is also the immediate assessment in the face-to-face meeting. A burglary detective who was unusually successful in obtaining confessions, describes his approach.

"If he is a street-hardened burglar, I am very friendly, very nice. I speak in a soft voice. If he has been arrested by a uniformed officer, I try to take a position on the suspect's side. 'I understand the uniformed officers were kind of heavy with you. You know how these young officers get sometimes.' I try to distance myself from the uniformed officers and from the police department, even though they know I'm a policeman. It works for me 90 percent of the time, especially if they had a verbal confrontation with the uniformed officers or didn't get along with them. It works to my advantage.

"I play up to them for a while, I'll act as if I'm the boss of the uniformed officers. My first interest is not the burglary. I'll take notes as to whether the uniformed officer was correct or not, they love that. I usually say that I'll deal with this officer later, 'However you realize I'll have to ask questions about this matter here.' In a very sympathetic manner, I keep my voice low, 'John I've got to talk about this burglary and theft allegation against you, however let's look at what the facts are.' I move in close to him for the first time. I'm on his side looking at police reports and the statements of witnesses.

"I stop and shake my head, being very sympathetic, I pause, I tell them at this point, 'Look you can see the facts here, you know them as well as I do, you know the district attorney will review them and I would like you to tell me your side of the story, so the D.A. doesn't have to depend on these other people.' I won't pause, I'll keep talking. 'It looks like they're going to file a case against you, but at least I can tell the D.A. why you got involved in this and I'll note your cooperation.'

"I'm continuing to distance myself from the system, although making sure I'm a policeman too. At this point most of the time I get a confession. I keep to the guidelines on the rules of evidence, and the confessions are not suppressed in court."

First-Offenders

"First-offenders are scared, and when I assess that frightened look on their face I make the most of it. It doesn't matter what socioeconomic level they're on, they're afraid and I usually get a very hardened, angry look on my face. I do not raise my voice, nor do I even let them think they're going to be physically harmed in any way, but if I can add to their discomfort level at that point, then that's what I intend to do. I don't ask questions, I tell them what they did based on statements I've obtained.

"Instead of asking whether they did the burglary, I tell them, 'You did the burglary, you know it and I know it.' I remind them that it's their first offense. I don't tell them I'll go easy on them, or anything that could suppress the confession in court, but it's my hope that by reminding them it's their first offense, that they will confess. If they start to talk I become more pleasant. The more they talk the more pleasant I get, even if it's only a partial confession.

" 'You're not that bad of a guy (or a woman). I know you didn't mean to do this.' Then I get the rest of the story. They want to be told you're not mad at them. Another line that works well if I'm still stumbling is, 'Can you give me something that I can tell the D.A. so that I can explain why you got involved in this crime. I know sometimes we're all hurting for money. I know you wouldn't normally have done this.' When I use the word 'we' I join myself with them. They like this. I'm giving them excuses that make it easier for them to confess.

"Normally I don't allow them to write out their own statements. I do it question and answer. Once they've started to talk it's important you keep the statement going, no pauses to give them a chance to think about deciding to stop the statement. Continuing to stay very close to them, sitting on top of them, once the statement has started, but not intimidating them, at first I never invade their territorial space because that causes animosity. Once we're friends I do that, that's all right.

"Another technique on first-offenders: 'I may be the best friend you've ever had in your entire life. I'm the one that's going to help you straighten out your entire life. If we succeed in this I know you'll never be in trouble again. You're not the criminal type.' If there are two or more suspects, but only one in the room, I will always blame it on the partner who isn't there. 'I know you wouldn't have done this if Bill hadn't talked you into it. You know they're going to try to lay the whole blame on you.'

"This is the divide and conquer technique. 'Your partner has completed a statement, he completely cooperated with us. I sure hope you don't miss the boat on this one.' Psychologically it's very difficult for a first-offender to remain silent or deny involvement when they know the co-conspirator has confessed, and implicated them. First-offenders are not aware that the statements of co-conspirators are not enough. We've got to have other evidence against them. It's very easy to get confessions from first-offender. They don't know the system."

Convicted Felons

"Burglars who've done time, will confess if the detective will take the time to review the case against them, point by point. The technique of being very friendly with the convicted felon is the best approach. The voice must be kept very low and very sympathetic. Once again, if you can criticize the police, the D.A. and the criminal justice system, they can relate to you better. For example, 'I can't stand the police department, but it keeps food on the table for the wife and kids.'

"Most of these people have loved ones and you're trying to alienate yourself from the police, even though they know you are the police.

The trickiest part about getting a confession from a convicted felon who's done time, is that they know they're going to do more time if they confess. So the technique that works the best is to tell them, 'You know you're going to have to do some more time on this case,' in a very low, sympathetic tone of voice.

"If they answer in the affirmative, by nodding the head or saying, 'Yeah I know I've got to do some time,' they'll confess to the entire crime at this point. The detective should not discuss the actual length of time they may serve in prison, because that may endanger the confession. Tell them, 'Why don't you take me out and show me all the houses you've burglarized, let's get it all done in one sweep.'

"When two or more suspects in a burglary are ordered in to speak to the detective, separate them, advise them of their Miranda rights and keep moving from one to another, using their statements against them. It's simple to get confessions under these conditions if they all show up at the same time. One will crack first.

"I do this by assessing the weakest one. I obtain a written statement from him and show it to the other suspects, one at a time. I make sure that the one who broke gives me the names of the others. I point out their name on the statement that their buddy has signed. Then they always confess.

"Women are tougher to crack if it is employer-related theft, but I think that if the detective is willing to spend a little bit more time, using the same techniques, she will confess.

"Probable cause for arrest warrants, for either men or women, is a tremendous tool the detective can use to obtain a confession, if used properly. The key to that is send the uniformed officer out to make the arrest, bring the suspect to the station, then immediately place him in a detention cell. Leave him in the cell for 30 to 45 minutes, then take him out and interview him. He is usually willing to talk to you. Advise him of his rights, show the warrant, and then he confesses."

Juvenile Offenders

"Juveniles present a different problem because of parental involvement. I have found taking the parents aside and convincing them of the guilt of the son or daughter is the best technique. That way, when the interview begins with the juvenile, the parents won't interfere. The juvenile will gain strength and confidence if his parents make one statement of verbal support to him during the interview so it is important that the parents don't talk, and this can only be accomplished if the parents are convinced beforehand of the guilt of their child.

"If the parents are convinced, then they can become a good tool for the detective, who can look the juvenile in the eye and tell him 'You know your parents know that you did this.' The detective is using the parents to his advantage when normally they just interfere. Continue to use the parents in the interview when the juvenile is caught in any lie, and request the parents to tell the child not to lie anymore. Use the parental pressure. If you win the parents, you'll win the child most of the time. Many detectives are intimidated by having the parents present, but the parents can be of help if this technique is used.

"Parents will not tolerate your yelling at their sons or daughters, so interviews with juveniles must be low key. If the parents join in in the interrogation and begin yelling at the son or daughter, the detective should be quiet and allow the parents to take it as far as they want to, and the detective should only join in for follow-up questions. This technique works very effectively."

General Comments

"Planning the interview is most important. Don't exhaust all the information you have in the first five minutes with the suspect. Save some facts to help push a reluctant suspect over the edge to a confession. When you show anger, let him read it in your eyes without raising your voice. If you catch him in a lie, shake your head, open your file read it for a while, put the file down, close it, then say 'You know that's not true.' If you catch him in what appears to be a lie, look him straight in the eyes and say, 'I can check on that.' Leave the room, come back in 15 minutes and tell him, 'No that's not correct, let's try it again.'

"Most suspects like to see the detective well dressed, not wearing a cheap shirt and tie, with a suit from the department store where they buy their clothing. Dress like a successful lawyer, it makes a lot of difference. Look very professional and successful. They must respect you to talk to you."

The Written Confession

After a suspect has confessed write out a simple short confession.
- Did you and Bill Smith commit a burglary to a house at 1750 Glencoe Street?
- How did you get in?
- What did you take?
- Where did you take the item?
- What did you do with it?
- You know the next question is going to deal with your motivation, why you committed this crime, answer this, Why did you do the burglary? Most detectives do not ask this question. The burglar will usually say "I needed the money" or "I heard they had a neat VCR."
- Did you realize you were committing a crime?
- Would you like to write something in your own handwriting that would help the judge and D.A. understand why you got involved in this crime?
- How many other burglaries did you commit?
- Did you make this statement of your own free will?
- Did you ask for an attorney, before or during this statement?
- Were any threats or promises made to you to obtain this statement?

In written statements do not go for too much detail. You do not want to know each and every thing the burglar did inside the home. There is no need to go into great detail. "Which drawer did you open next; which papers did you touch; did you lift up the typewriter?" Such questions can lead to difficulty in the courtroom and serve no useful purpose. Additional questions may be needed to the 12 given above, for example, a youth who was asked how he got in a house replied "Through the door with a key that was left with my dad." He was then asked "Did you have permission to use the key? Did you have permission to enter the house?"

Additional questions are needed for special items taken such as a car and credit cards. "Did you take the Gordon's Datsun car? Did you wreck it in Byers, Colorado? Did you take credit cards; did you use them to purchase anything?"

The Burglar's Visiting Card

Whenever questioning the victim or the suspect in a case of burglary, care should be taken to ask about the burglar's visiting card. A delicate regard for the feelings of others on matters excremental, all too often leads to concealment of this information. A small number of burglars leave a very distinctive trademark at the scene of the crime. They have a bowel motion outside the home, in their pants as they are breaking in or inside the home. They may make their deposit in the toilet and then fail to flush the bowl. More often, it is in a place that is most likely to distress the householder, for example on the dining room table. The table has to be replaced, because each meal brings a reminder of the unwelcome and unappetizing gift.

A smell of detergent at a burglary scene should remind the patrol officer to ask whether the burglar left his visiting card, because often victims will clean up the mess before calling the police. If the burglar had an accident in his pants, he may wash himself and leave his underpants in the trash can. The patrol officer should ask his partner to check the underpants, because the burglar may have wiped himself with his parole papers.

This distressing occupational hazard is not confined to nervous, inexperienced burglars. Career criminals have complained to John about this problem. Just when they are ready to break into a home they have to stop and have a bowel motion, even though they had one before starting their day's work. A burglar, with the first name Ernest, was called "Crapping Ernie" because of this awkward habit. The detective who first asks a suspect whether he leaves his visiting card at the scene of his crime, may find that asking this question establishes a bond with the suspect. A secret has been shared.

Theft by Employees

There are often many possible suspects in cases of theft by an employee. Polygraph testing is a good method of identifying the offender or offenders. The polygraph examiner might ask each subject:

- Do you have any idea who might have committed this offense? The truthful subject may identify some suspects and give his reasons. For example, he may list only those people who had access to the stolen items. The lying subject may not name anyone, or he may say that it could have been anyone, including customers.
- Is there anyone that you feel did not commit the offense? The truthful subject will volunteer names, and once again he will give his reasons. The lying subject may not vouch for anyone. He wants as many people as possible to be under suspicion.
- Do you think that the offense was committed deliberately? The truthful subject will probably say yes, and he will give his reasons. The lying subject will say that the missing items could have been lost or mislaid.
- Could your fingerprints be found at the scene of the offense? The truthful person will give a direct answer, yes or no, and will not be concerned if indeed his fingerprints could have been at the scene. The lying subject is likely to give long explanations and qualified answers to explain why his fingerprints might be found at the scene of the crime.
- Have you ever thought of doing something like this, even though you didn't commit this offense? The truthful person will usually deny ever having had such thoughts. The lying subject is more

likely to say that he has thought about it, but add that he did
not do it.

• What should happen to the person if he is caught? The truthful
subject is likely to suggest prompt substantial punishment, especially as the offender has caused so much inconvenience to other
employees. The lying subject is likely to make excuses for the
guilty person and to suggest mild punishment.

CHECK AND CREDIT CARD OFFENSES

The pen is mightier than the sword.

Insufficient Fund and No Account Checks

A sympathetic approach is recommended toward the suspect who
writes a check knowing that there are insufficient funds in the
account to cover the check and also toward the suspect who writes
a check on an account that has been closed. These offenders try to
excuse, rather than deny, their wrongdoing when the detective
does not show a stern attitude, but one of understanding. Even
though the suspect may have protested his or her innocence to the
arresting officer, a confession can often be obtained relatively
quickly.

A woman, who wrote a check for $163.82 to pay for groceries,
was arrested at the supermarket after a telephone call to the bank
showed that the bank had no account in her name. She told the
officer who responded that she had made a deposit in her account
that day, but she did not have the deposit receipt with her. Another
telephone call to the bank showed that her account had been closed
one year previously and any teller would have refused her deposit.
After sympathetic questioning by a detective she stated:

"Yes, I wrote a check because we did not have food or nothing
in the house. My check from work I used it for rent. I live with my
sister. She has two kids and I have two kids. They were hungry
and we were hungry. I figured write the check and then on Friday
I get my check from work and I'll pay it. I told the officer I made

a deposit in the bank but I didn't. I told him that because I was scared. I did not know the account was closed because me and my husband are getting a divorce. Maybe he knew about it, but I didn't know. I guess I got carried away. My sister is also getting a divorce, we had no one to turn to. It's hard trying to raise two kids by myself. All I have to say is I am very sorry. I know I did wrong."

Stolen and Counterfeit Checks and Credit Cards

The man who buys a blank check or money order from a burglar may make it payable to himself. When arrested, he will claim he was having a garage sale, and a stranger gave him the check as payment for some item; or that he sold something to a man he met in a park; or that he helped a man load a truck. These suspects should be questioned in detail about the alleged payment to them for goods or services. Usually they have thought up some explanation but not the fine details of who, when, where and so on.

For example, a long distance truck driver who lived in California was arrested in Denver for cashing a stolen money order made out to himself. He claimed that it was for helping a man in Ohio, and that the check was mailed to him in Denver. When asked for his mailing address in Denver, he gave a non-existent address.

This form of interrogation should also be used when a person is caught using a stolen credit card, perhaps purchased from a burglar and claiming that a casual acquaintance told him that he could use it as payment for some item, favor or labor.

Ring operations, in which four or five team members under the control of a leader obtain cash advances from banks using counterfeit credit cards, along with counterfeit identification, provide special problems for the detective. Plastic credit cards are stolen and then embossed with the names of people who have large balances in their bank accounts. The number listed on the counterfeit credit card will be their correct credit card account number, so that the company will authorize large cash advances. This information is obtained from accomplices employed in large banks. If a team member is arrested, he will insist that he is the person listed on his credit card and on his ID.

The team leader will arrange for the team member's quick release on bond. This person will immediately fly back to the state where he lives. If his fingerprints are not on file with the FBI, it may be impossible to discover his identity. It is important, therefore, to obtain from him as much information as possible that might later lead to his arrest. Often these people are not prepared for such detailed questioning and some correct information may be supplied, or if it is false information, it may still provide useful clues. For example, when asked for their Social Security number, they may give their true number but transpose two of the digits. The following information should be obtained:

- Name, nickname, alias, address, telephone number.
- Date and place of birth.
- Social Security number.
- The name, address, and phone number of spouse, father, mother, father-in-law, mother-in-law, children, defense attorney, or other person the subject can be contacted through in an emergency.
- Military service, branch of service, military service number, selective service number, selective service board and address, dates of active duty, date of discharge, type of discharge, VA claim number, disability claimed.
- Automobile, description, tag number, tag registration, state and year.
- INS alien number, date of entry, port of entry.
- Bank checking and savings accounts, number, name and location of bank.
- Charge accounts, credit cards, organizations.
- Hobbies/skills, places frequented, last school attended.
- Previous addresses and dates, schools attended by children.
- Dates of employment, name and address of employer, duties performed.

Ring operations may also use four or five team members under the control of a leader to cash a large number of counterfeit checks over a weekend and then leave town. The rings avoid personal checks and use large businesses, such as a supermarket chain, federal, state, county, and city government checks as well as cashier's checks, which can be used to purchase vehicles. The method of interrogation is the same as for ring use of counterfeit credit cards.

Fraudulent Application for Credit Cards or Checks

The skillful offender travels to a distant city, checks old newspapers for deaths of a newborn infant around the time of his own birth, and obtains a death certificate by claiming that he is an attorney doing research on an estate. Then he obtains the birth certificate from information on the death certificate and acquires a personal identification in this person's name. He opens a savings account and a personal checking account. He takes out a small loan from a credit union in which he has a savings account, thereby establishing a credit rating. Finally, he obtains local then major credit cards.

He is now ready to make many major purchases using his credit cards. Alternatively he may use his checks for the same purpose. Items such as computers or cars are sold and he quickly leaves town. He may take valuable merchandise with him and dispose of it elsewhere. It may be very difficult to trace this type of offender. The best method of interrogation is to confront him with all the evidence against him. "Gregory, you are history, this is what we've got on you. We've got you cold. The only person who can help you is yourself. We've got a couple of loose ends we need to tie up, we're interested in how you . . ."

No promises are made, but the suspect realizing that conviction is inevitable, may assume that if he cooperates with the detective, he will receive some help when the time comes for sentencing.

Chapter 10
DRUG OFFENSES AND INFORMANTS

There are two ways of being addicted to heroin. One way is to mainline it. The other is to traffic in it.
Richard Berdin, *Code Name Richard*

Illegal drugs and crime go hand in hand. Drug offenders commit crimes to obtain drugs, or to obtain money to buy drugs. They break the law by cultivating marijuana, by manufacturing drugs and by smuggling illicit drugs into the country. They murder or otherwise treat unkindly informants as well as those who either steal their drugs or fail to pay for them. The illegal use of drugs is so widespread that all suspects should be questioned about drug use.

One should start with inquiries about the use of marijuana, because abuse is so common and the criminal penalties are so light. Once the suspect has admitted using marijuana, it becomes easier for him to admit the use of other drugs. Inquire about the main classes of drugs. The depth of your inquiries will depend on the circumstances and your level of suspicion.

Marijuana and hashhish

Street names include charas, ganga, grass, griffa, hemp, herb, Mary Jane, Maui wowie, mutah, Panama red, pot, reefer, skunk weed, smoke, Thai sticks and weed. A marijuana cigarette is a joint; the butt is a roach; a puff is a toke; and an ounce of marijuana is a lid.

Inhalants
Juvenile offenders should be asked whether they sniff glue, plastic cement or aerosol sprays — "the grocery store high."

Down-and-out street people, especially those with paint on their fingers or around the mouth, should be asked whether they sniff paint, paint thinner, gasoline, lighter fluid, spot remover or fingernail polish.

Gays may inhale "poppers and snappers," amyl and butyl nitrites.

Some groups inhale nitrous oxide (laughing gas) or ether.

Hallucinogens
LSD (acid, California sunshine, microdots) PCP (angel dust, crystal, DOA, dust, embalming fluid, hog, killer weed, rocket fuel, supergrass, superweed and surfer).

Peyote, mescaline (big chief, buttons, cactus), psilocybin (magic mushrooms and simple Simon) and other hallucinogens.

Depressants
Barbiturates (barbs, downers), Amytal (blue birds, blues), Nembutal (nembies, yellow jackets, yellows), Seconal (reds), Tuinal (christmas trees, double trouble).

Quaaludes ('ludes), Sopor (soapers, sopes).

Valium (mother's helper, val), Librium, Equanil, Miltown, Doriden.

Stimulants
Cocaine (blow, 'caine, coke, crack, girl, gold dust, lady, line, mujer, nose candy, paradise, perico, rock, snow and toot)

Amphetamines (speed), Benzedrine (bennies, hearts), Dexedrine (dexies, copilots, hearts), Methedrine (meth, speed), also black beauties, crosses, purple hearts, truck drivers and uppers.

Narcotics

Heroin (boy, junk, smack, stuff, tar), morphine (M, Miss Emma, monkey, morph), Dilaudid (D's, dillies, lords), Demerol, Percodan (percs), methadone (meth), Darvon, Talwin, codeine and other narcotics

The person who admits to using any of these drugs can be asked about his source of supply and his knowledge of the drug culture. The citizen who appears to be under the influence of alcohol, but has no smell of alcohol on his breath can be asked: Are you on medication; are you sick; are you diabetic; are you epileptic? If he says no to all these questions, he can be asked if he has taken any drugs. Does he know anybody using illegal drugs? Does he know a lot of people using drugs? If he says, "Yes, everybody does it," then obviously he is part of the drug culture.

The person who is found in possession of a small amount of marijuana knows that in most jurisdictions today this is a misdemeanor offense. He knows that the charge is not serious. He is not likely to reveal information on his dealer to the officer in the hope of receiving favorable consideration in court. If an effort is made to interrogate him, he will probably freeze up. A friendly approach, however, on the part of the officer may be productive.

If the man is on probation for drug offenses, or if he is found in possession of speed, cocaine, heroin or a larger amount of marijuana, then he should be taken to the police building for questioning by a narcotics detective.

He can be asked where he is getting his dope. "How many dealers do you know? I don't want any specifics. I don't want your connect (main supplier)." Most users have one main supplier and two or three alternate suppliers in case the connect is not available. The approach is low key. The suspect may be willing to inform on one of his alternate suppliers. One man even revealed his dealer's source of supply. The detective cannot make any promises in return for information, but he can say that he will tell the district attorney that the defendant cooperated in the investigation.

The detective, as in any questioning, should have a respectful attitude and not talk down to these persons. It is helpful to empathize with them. You understand that they have a drug problem. "It's like an illness, it is an illness; it's hard to kick it."

Even if he is unwilling to talk about his dealers, he may be willing to talk about people on the street who are involved, as he probably is himself, in shoplifting, check and credit card offenses and burglaries. Burglars know burglars, they have pride in their profession and like to talk about their skills. Encourage them to do so. They may even provide information on a fence that has not treated them well.

It is most important to warn them not to tell their public defender that they have been providing information to the police, because there is the risk that the public defender may reveal this information in talking to his other clients, with awkward consequences for the informants.

DRUG OFFENDER PROFILES

There is special need for caution in using the profiles of drug offenders. The profiles are usually no more than descriptions of the typical behavior of these offenders as they go about their business; and the way they go about their business may not be the same in Miami as it is in Denver, and it may not be the same one year as it is the following year. Drug offenders tend to learn from their mistakes. Furthermore, some of them become aware of new police tactics and modify their behavior to avoid detection. Keep in mind that criminal profiles are derived from study of those offenders who have been arrested. The reason some drug offenders escape arrest, may be because they do not fit the profile.

The street dealer or "bag man," who is often a drug abuser himself, will show the telltale signs of drug abuse. He obtains his drugs from the "ounce man," who in turn obtains his drugs from the "pound man." Upper echelon dealers are probably not drug abusers and do not want their lieutenants to use drugs. They realize that drug abuse increases the likelihood of the lieutenant cheating them by cutting (diluting) the drug still further in order to keep some for himself and increases the risk of his being arrested, with the danger that he may become an informer for the police.

Upper echelon dealers do not sell drugs on the street. They may be well dressed, of neat appearance, with open neck shirts and expensive gold chains around the neck. They handle large amounts of drugs. In contrast, the bag man obtains relatively small amounts for sale to his customers on the street.

Profiles of Street Dealers and Drug Abusers

- Unkempt appearance, unshaven, uncombed hair, dirty clothes, poor physical hygeine. Even a low-level street dealer may wear designer jeans, possibly with the price tag still on them, that have been boosted by one of his customers and provided in part payment for drugs. Tennis shoes and dark glasses with dark frames (but not mirror glasses) are fashionable among many street dealers.

- No bulge in back pocket of trousers. Street criminals do not carry identification on them, so there is not the usual bulge of a wallet in the back pocket of their jeans. The drug abuser on the street may have a boosting list in his pocket, because he has difficulty remembering the orders of his customers. The list may include, "Leona size 14 dress, Jimmy waist 32, length 30". He may also have a name and address book that contains a wealth of information, providing the detective can recognize the nicknames.

- Unhealthy, malnourished appearance, looks older than he or she really is.

- Possibly tattoos, especially "joint" tattoos, on hands. Tattoos elsewhere may be covered by clothing. Injection marks, bruises at injection sites and tracks (a scar along the path of a vein from repeated injections), may be hidden by make-up, especially in the case of female offenders.

- The street dope dealer just stands around, waiting for his customers. In order not to be conspicuous he may wait at a bus stop, but he does not get on any bus. Often his drugs are hidden nearby, perhaps behind the bumper of a car that does not belong to him, or in a packet of cigarettes hidden under some trash or behind a pillar. He remains close to his stash, looks at it, and walks toward it from time to time. The drugs may be held in his hand so that they can be quickly swallowed in an emergency, or in his mouth so that when you speak to him, his voice is not sharp and distinct. When his speech is muffled, look inside his mouth.

- The street dealer avoids the police. He stands close to buildings and walks down alleys or between buildings whenever the police appear, so that he has a head start if the police come after him. There may be momentary eye contact, but if the officer looks in the rearview mirror of the police car as he drives away, he will see that the suspected drug dealer is watching him closely.

- The street dealer, when questioned by a police officer, has no identification, no driver's license, no living relative anywhere, no Social Security number, and will say that he has never been arrested before, despite the presence of "joint tattoos." The birthdate and age that he gives may not match.

- The person who is using speed will be nervous, very paranoid, very talkative and may have rapid eye movement. He can be friendly one moment and belligerent the next moment. He is probably carrying a concealed weapon. Cocaine abusers can also be very paranoid and can become very violent. The heroin abuser is not paranoid, just cautious. While on heroin he is mellow and sleepy. His pupils are small and his head droops (this is referred to as "going on the nod"). Signs of withdrawal from heroin include depression, restlessness, diarrhea, anxiety, yawning, watery eyes, runny nose, chills, tremors and dilated pupils. A person high on LSD may be extremely anxious, disoriented and troubled by hallucinations. His statements may be irrational, reflecting his world of fantasy. There may be sudden acts of violence. The person using PCP can be just as bizarre in his statements and behavior, but he is much more dangerous. One minute he may just stare at others and say nothing. A short time later he may become very aggressive and assault anyone near him. Because his sensation of pain is reduced and because of his wild excitement, it may be extremely difficult to restrain him. Physical signs can include coughing and wheezing and jerky eye movements (nystagmus).

- He may have on him drug paraphernalia: a needle, perhaps in his sock; a spoon, cotton, a little bottle of water, and a syringe; rolling paper; snow seals; roach clip; or tooters-tubes.

Profile of the Drug Dependent Nurse

- Prefers 11 PM to 7 AM duty period because fewer staff are on duty and there are more requests for sedative drugs by patients.
- Arrives early for work because she needs a fix, but some nurse addicts are frequently late for work.
- Wears long-sleeved uniform or sweater, even in summer, to hide needle marks or tracks.
- Many physical complaints, headaches, back pain and fatigue. Much sick time off work.
- Prominent weight loss, looks sick.
- After self-injection of Demerol or other opiates she has glazed look, shows poor concentration, and her notes in patient charts are poorly written or illegible.
- Scratches out and rewrites medication doses. There are errors in charting narcotic medications.
- Often comes to ward on her day off to get something from her locker, or because "she thought" there was a training meeting, but she comes to pilfer drugs from the narcotics cabinet or from the operating room.
- Has frequent changes of employment because hospitals ask her to resign. She is not fired because the hospital wishes to avoid bad publicity.
- If arrested, she changes her name, in case the hospital where she seeks employment checks her police record.

Profile of the Air Courier

- Gives false or non-existent call-back telephone number when making telephone reservation for flight.
- Pays cash for the ticket as he wishes to avoid leaving a paper trail.
- Travels and buys ticket under false name, changes name after buying the ticket.
- May arrive at airport with another drug courier, later acts as if he does not know this person, yet exchanges glances and in other ways betrays mutual acquaintance.
- Avoids direct flight from Miami, Los Angeles or other drug source city to destination. Changes airline at intermediate stop. Prefers early morning or late evening arrival, as narcotics officers less likely to be on duty at these times.
- Luggage identification tags, required by the Federal Aviation Administration, contain little information, no information or false name. He is overly protective of his luggage.
- The first or last to leave the airplane on arrival. May even wait 10 minutes before leaving plane in the hope that detectives will have left the concourse. May be asked to leave the plane because he is waiting in it so long.
- Loose fitting or bulky clothing to hide possession of packages of drugs.
- Cocaine cowboys like to flaunt their wealth, a Rolex watch, expensive gold chains around the neck and casual but expensive designer clothes.
- The mule who has been hired for one trip may have inexpensive clothing, yet have a very expensive briefcase.
- Alert watchful appearance as he leaves the plane, continues to look at others as he walks down the concourse. Very nervous, may sweat profusely.
- The body carrier who has condoms of cocaine in his stomach or intestines will pass gas loudly and repeatedly as he walks down the concourse.
- Almost runs down the concourse or walks conspicuously slowly.
- May go directly to a telephone to make a call, or may go to a

toilet to meet the person who will pick up the drugs and pay him.
- At baggage carousel he stands back, rather than waiting to pick up his baggage the moment it arrives.
- Even when leaving airport he looks over his shoulder to see if anyone is following him.

Law enforcement officers at major airports receive training on the legal guidelines for stopping, questioning and searching people who fit a drug courier profile. These special procedures, which should be followed meticulously in order to avoid trouble in the courtroom, will not be reviewed in this book. Mention has not been made of some features of the drug courier profile at the request of the Stapleton International Airport Narcotics Unit.

Profile of Drug Smuggling Aircraft

- Passenger seats removed.
- Numerous cardboard boxes, trash bags, duffel bags or other containers inside the aircraft.
- Fuel containers such as large drums, fuel cans and rubber bladders inside the cabin.
- Factory-installed long range fuel tanks.
- Aircraft windows covered by curtains or tape.
- Windows altered to permit airdropping of drugs.
- Undersurface of airplane and propellers pitted from landing on roads or dirt airstrips.
- Aircraft registration number false or altered.
- Aircraft parked long way from airport office, alongside motor home or pickup with camper body and ground to air radio equipment. Brief landing to meet these vehicles or to refuel.
- Odor of perfume to hide smell of marijuana.
- Cash payment for fuel and services.
- Pilot does not leave plane unattended during servicing, may request map of Florida or Mexico. There may be maps of Mexico, Colombia or Caribbean islands inside the aircraft.
- Pilot or passengers reluctant to show identification or to discuss

places of origin and destination.
- Aircraft flying or landing after dark without lights.
- Arrives extremely low on fuel.

Profile of Drug Smuggling Mother Ship

- Vessel's name and homeport not visible or sloppily painted on the stern and on removable boards on both sides of the pilot house.
- No nationality or registry flag when first sighted.
- Vessel in poor condition—rusty hull, cracking or peeling paint, possible hull damage.
- More radio and radar antennae than would be expected.
- No fishing gear visible on fishing vessel, no nets or boards to get the nets down, new but unused fishing equipment, or rusty fishing gear that appears not to have been used for a long time.
- Not sailing in usual shipping lanes or fishing grounds.
- False waterline, so that the vessel looks high in the water, as if it is not loaded with marijuana.
- Extra fuel drums on deck.
- Hatches padlocked.
- Unnatural crew reaction to surveillance by plane—instead of showing interest in the plane and waving, crew members disappear or do not even look at the plane.
- No running lights at night.
- Marijuana bales on deck or odor of marijuana.
- Erratic course change after sighting by Coast Guard helicopter.
- Painting vessel a different color and changing name of vessel after helicopter leaves the area—in some cases have still been painting when the Coast Guard cutter alerted by the helicopter arrived.
- Failure to respond to radio contact—claims radio or compass problems (Macdonald and Kennedy).

Profiles do not usually refer to the vessel's name, which may be conventional, but often the names suggest sexual activity (*Orgasm*

III, Hooker) or a connection with drugs *(Snow Flake, Mary Jane* and *Happy Times).*

Profile of Drug Courier and His Vehicle

The profile varies from one part of the U.S. to another and from year to year. Previously the drug courier was often a poorly dressed young man, who looked as if he could not buy gasoline for the large, new, expensive, four-door car that he was driving. When asked how to contact the owner of the car, he would give an evasive or implausible answer. He would often have a false driver's license or false papers for the car. Even if his papers were in order, he would be quick to sign a consent form for the police to search his car.

Previously drug couriers often used rental cars, with out-of-state license plates, especially from Florida or California. Today the drug courier is likely to be driving his own car, and he will not look out of place in the car. He will have a legitimate driver's license as well as the proper registration papers for the car. He will not permit the police to search his car unless they have a search warrant. The following features have been noted on the cocaine corridors between Florida and New York or California.

- Older, full-size car, registered in the name of the driver. The dealer loses less money if the police seize an older less expensive car that is being used by one of his couriers. Some cars have a scanner and a CB radio, so the driver can listen to truck drivers reporting the locations of police vehicles on the highway.
- Young male driver and young male companion. They may have expensive but casual clothing and gold jewelry. Young Hispanic couples with small children in the car are less likely to arouse suspicion. They will say that they are visiting relatives in a different part of the U.S. than their hometown.
- Drives carefully at or below the speed limit, unlike most drivers on interstate highways, but may exceed the speed limit in order to avoid arousing the suspicion of officers on the lookout for drug couriers. He may be weaving if he has been sampling his

cargo or if he is tired from long distance driving without sleep.
- May be driving between 7 PM and 4:30 AM.
- Keeps careful eye on any patrol car visible in his rearview mirror, or driver may drive by highway patrol car and not look at it.
- Pays cash for gasoline.
- The amateur courier, if involved in an accident, may be more concerned about his briefcase, than the major damage to his new $12,000 vehicle. The professional would be unlikely to be carrying his drugs in a briefcase.
- Perfume, fabric softner or air freshener to hide smell of marijuana.
- Nervousness, sweating, chain smoking when questioned.
- Spare tire or jack inside the car may mean that drugs take up all the space in the trunk. The professional drug courier will not make such an obvious blunder. His drugs are hidden in the spare tire, in specially concealed compartments in the doors, below the floor of the trunk or elsewhere, in the gas tank, spare gas tank, or in the sewage tank of a motor home.

INTERVIEWING INFORMANTS

The business I'm in right now, you can't get life insurance.

Confidential Informant

Confidential informants play an important role in helping police to solve all forms of major crime. Over 90 percent of confidential informants are criminals, who gave their first information in the hope of avoiding either arrest or prosecution. Some scoundrels would betray their own mothers to avoid going to jail, but there are criminals who are unwilling to squeal on their partners. The interviewing skills and persuasive powers of the detective may win the day. Once an offender has provided information, it is easier for him to do it again later, for money or for other favors.

Other criminals from the beginning provide information for money. Some offenders inform because: they like an officer, they want to return a favor, they want attention, they want revenge on another criminal, or they want to eliminate competition by putting a rival drug dealer in the penitentiary. Jealousy can be a motive. When a burglar leaves his girlfriend for another woman, she may inform because he cannot see her when he is in jail.

The informant may want immediate payment of $50 for information on a drug deal. Tell him it's C.O.D.—cash on delivery. There is no payment until his information is proved to be accurate. Question him in detail about the suspect, his home and his activities. Verify this information. Use the usual interviewing techniques to see if he is lying to you. Ask him about the street price for a gram of cocaine or a hit of acid. If he quotes a figure that is way above or below the usual amount, he is probably blowing hot air. Improbable claims ("He has 80 sawed-off shotguns in his home.") arouse immediate suspicion.

Do not show him a mug shot of the suspect and say, "Is that him?" Instead show him a group of mug shots, including one of the suspect, and ask him if he recognizes anyone. Check all the information he has provided, but keep in mind that these people may forget dates, mistake one apartment for another and not recognize the need for absolute accuracy on important matters. Drive him out to the suspect's house and get him to identify it and the suspect's car.

His report that the suspect is a drug dealer may be correct, but he may not know whether the suspect presently has drugs in his home. Yet he may say that the drugs are there. There is the risk that he will plant the drugs under a couch on a visit to the house. The genuineness of the suspect's outrage upon his arrest should warn the detective of what happened. It is important to impress on the informant that he must not set anybody up for arrest—there can be no entrapment. He must not suggest an armed robbery to another crook and after the robbery offer to reveal the name of the robber in return for $50.

The most important thing in dealing with informants is to control them. The detective has to be in control of the interview, the informant has to be truthful, the informant must not be involved in any felonies, and the informant must not deceive the detective.

"We expect you to tell us the truth, not what you think we want to hear. Don't give us bad information, don't withhold information, or you may get burned. Remember we know a little more than you think we do. If we catch you in a lie, you're through. Any deal is off if you get involved in a felony."

If he does not have any information on narcotics, ask him about burglaries, forgeries, credit card offenses, robberies, sexual assaults and homicides. Does he know anyone who is wanted by the police? He may not have any useful information, but in the future he may be of assistance. It is hard work keeping in touch with informants. You have to telephone them frequently. You have to be prepared to help them out at any time. They may call you at any hour.

Many of these people are like children, they seem unable to cope with the demands of everyday life: paying traffic tickets, requesting installation of a telephone, planning ahead financially and so on. You almost have to adopt some of them. The policy of not paying any money until useful information has been obtained does not apply to subjects who have been helpful over a long period of time. "Could I borrow $5 for the baby, we don't have no diapers," may mean $5 out of the detective's pocket. You make a long-term commitment to these people.

In summary, avoid referring to him in derogatory terms. Do not use the words snitch or informant. Don't hurry him when you are talking to him, but keep the conversation from wandering. Sympathize with him over any difficulties he may be having. Show appreciation for information of value. Do not belittle worthless information. Press for details. Take notes or make a record of information as soon as possible. Avoid questions that reveal what you already know. Avoid questions that embarrass him. Control him.

Chapter 11
ARSON
AND BOMBING

It is most unwise for an insured person to have more than one fire in his own name.

Howard Dearden, *The Fire Raisers*

ARSON

The crime of arson poses special problems for the fire investigator: physical evidence pointing to arson may be destroyed in the fire; the use of a time delay device enables the firesetter to be miles from the crime scene at the time of the fire; there are a wide variety of motives for arson; and there may be no clues linking the arsonist, especially the pyromanic or compulsive firesetter, to his crime. The detective should keep in mind not only the criminal profiles of likely firesetters, but also the many motives for arson.

Motives

Financial Gain

Fires are set to destroy outdated machinery, outmoded merchandise, buildings that have been condemned and buildings that can neither be rented nor sold. On a more modest scale, a homeowner can refurnish his living room with the insurance payment for a small "accidental fire." Heirs to an estate who want a quick cash distribution but are unable to sell the family home can burn it.

Intimidation

Union activists can intimidate non-union builders and construction contractors into hiring only union labor by burning down large condominium and apartment house complexes before roofing and insulation have been installed. Anti-abortion groups can discourage abortion clinics from continuing to operate by firebombing the premises.

Vandalism

Children, youths and vagrants obtain pleasure from setting fire to schools, vacant buildings and other property.

Revenge

Discarded lovers gain revenge by burning the vehicles, possessions or homes of their former partners. Employees with a grievance, indeed any person with a strong sense of resentment, can light a match.

Concealment of Other Crimes

Burglary, theft and homicide can be concealed by burning down a building. The burglar hopes that the theft of valuable electronic equipment will not be noticed, and the murderer hopes that the death of his victim from a gunshot wound will be attributed to the effects of the fire. Account books are destroyed by fire near tax time in order to defraud the IRS.

Homicide

Fires are set to kill people.

Suicide

A surprising number of suicidal persons choose this method to end their lives, but relatively few succeed. The person who attempts to asphyxiate himself by sticking his head in an oven and turning the gas on may change his mind. If he then lights a cigarette, there can be a violent explosion and a fire.

Need for Attention

Fires provide the arsonist an opportunity to obtain attention by calling the fire department to report the fire, by saving someone from a burning building or by helping the firemen put out the fire. Volunteer firemen have set fires in order to demonstrate their skill or to show off some new piece of equipment.

Security guards, fearful of being laid off because of a financial recession affecting business, or in order to attract favorable attention, may set a fire, then report it and attempt to put it out. The guard may say that he saw someone running from the scene and chased him. He may give a very detailed description, even to the color of the man's eyes, yet he was never closer to the man than 150 feet. The guard may have a dirty uniform and an unshaven appearance or he may be dressed as neatly as any police officer. Often such a guard is a frustrated police officer who has failed the entrance examination for the police department.

Compulsion to Set Fires—Pyromania

There are few compulsive firesetters, but they set many fires and continue to do so over many years. These offenders gain release of tension and a feeling of excitement, often sexual excitement, from their fires. Often they set fire to any building in sight to meet their need for excitement, but they can also pick specific targets to satisfy more conventional motives, for example, to seek revenge on an employer or to obtain money from an insurance company by burning their own property. They can also work for terrorist groups who appreciate their expertise.

Terrorism

Terrorist groups set fires to destroy property, to intimidate opponents and to draw attention to their cause.

There may be more than one motive. For example, a juvenile delinquent may burn a neighbor's house for a thrill, to conceal a burglary and for revenge. A delusional schizophrenic patient may set a fire for bizarre motives. He may, for example, burn down a church to purge it of evil and to please the Lord.

QUESTIONING WITNESSES

When arson is suspected, the detective should interview the person who turns in the alarm. There may be people at the fire scene, especially those most eager to help the firefighters, who should also be questioned. Special circumstances suggest special questions, but in general the following questions should be asked:
- What did you see?
- When did you first see fire or smoke?
- Where did you first see fire or smoke?
- What was the color of the flames? Did the color change? What was the color of the smoke? Did the color change? Expert fire investigators can tell detectives the conclusions that can be drawn from answers to these questions.
- Where did you see the flames? Fire burning in more than one location suggests arson.
- Did you smell any unusual odors (such as gasoline)?
- Did you see anyone leaving the building?
- Did you see any vehicles leaving the scene?
- Did you see anyone acting suspiciously?

QUESTIONING FIREFIGHTERS

Firefighters should be asked the above questions. They are usually better informants on the color of the flames and smoke. They should also be asked:
- The license numbers of vehicles parked near the fire scene.
- The presence of familiar faces in the crowd. Firesetters like to admire their handiwork, so they stay at the scenes of their fires.
- The names of persons eager to volunteer their services.
- The names of people treated for smoke inhalation or burns.

Firesetters often insist on helping the firefighters and may be admitted to hospital for treatment of burns or smoke inhalation. A burned victim or heroic rescuer may be the arsonist. Often a firesetter will grossly exaggerate his injuries or exposure to smoke.

- Was there any evidence of breaking and entering, such as a torn window screen, broken window or pry marks on an entrance door?
- Were burglar alarms, fire alarms or sprinkler systems inactivated? Were hydrants blocked?
- Were entrances or corridors blocked to obstruct the work of the firefighter?
- Were fire doors held open to hasten the spread of the fire? Were holes punched in the walls to allow for better cross ventilation and to facilitate the lateral movement of fire? (O'Connor).
- Were there clues to arson, such as gasoline cans, paint thinner cans, timing devices, melted candle wax, trailers (to aid in the spread of the fire), discarded matches in unusual places, gas burners in the ON position, disconnected gas pipes?
- Were normal contents of homes such as television sets, clothing, family pictures or other items of sentimental value missing? Was a gun cabinet empty? Were normal contents of businesses, such as computers and typewriters, missing?
- Were the contents of a room rearranged to assist the fire?
- If the owner of the home or building was at the scene, did he appear to be upset over the damage to his property; did he show signs of nervousness? How did he learn that his property was on fire, and what was his opinion on the cause of the fire?

The manager of a business destroyed by fire did not seem at all upset about the fire. His first remark was "We have been having electrical problems." When told that it was not an electrical fire, he said, "It must have been a cigarette then."

In the Aetna Life and Casualty Company report, *Detecting Arson: What the Firefighter Should Do*, King suggests the following questions on the interior of the building:

- Does the fire appear to be in separate locations, with no apparent connection?

- Is the fire moving in an irregular manner or in an unusual direction, i.e., horizontally along the baseboard, down a staircase instead of up, or "walking" across the floor?
- Do the flames react abnormally to the water from the hoseline? (Straight streams ordinarily "darken down" the fire immediately, but if a flammable liquid is present, the flames will tend to spread in different directions, as if being pushed by the water. If a fog stream is used, the fire tends to reflash wherever flammable liquid is present.)
- Is more water than normal required to put out this fire?
- Does the water react violently when applied to the fire?
- Were any extinguishing agents, other than water, needed to put out the fire?

QUESTIONING THE OWNER

- Tell me everything you know about the fire.
- How did you learn about the fire, from whom and at what time?
- What, in your opinion, was the cause of the fire?
- Do you know anyone who might have set the fire—vandals, neighbors, personal enemies, former friends, former employees, competitors, disgruntled customers? When items of great sentimental value are placed together and set on fire, it is important to think of revenge and to ask about former lovers. If the victim is gay or lesbian, the question about former friends is especially important.
- Has there been any malfunction in the furnace, water heater, stove, gas or electrical system; if so, who made repairs and when?
- Were there any flammable liquids in the building? If so, the nature, amount and where stored?
- Names of insurance company and agent? Any recent increase in coverage?
- Any previous fires? If so, location, name of insurance company, policy number, amount claimed and received?
- Is there anything else you would like to add?

Arson for Profit

When arson for profit is suspected, the detective will ask the owner of a business who was the last person to leave and lock the business; who informed him of the fire; who has keys to the building; and has he had any union or labor problems? An effort will be made to obtain answers to the following questions from businessmen, particularly business associates, in the community.

- Is the owner planning to retire?
- Has the business been advertised for sale?
- Has there been any recent cancellation of orders?
- Has there been any court judgment against the company?
- Are there any new business competitors?
- Is the machinery outdated and in need of replacement?
- Is the merchandise in stock out of fashion or unlikely to be sold for any other reason?
- Has there been any recent termination of lease?
- Has there been any failure to meet mortgage or other payments?
- Is the owner in financial difficulty?

One approach to conceal that the owner may become a suspect, which might put him on guard, is to say, "The insurance company will touch base with us, we'll have to ask some questions in order to expedite your insurance company payment. We often have to satisfy the insurance company that you are not involved in this." Then ask the above questions, and also when was the property acquired, what was the price, down payment, mortgage or mortgages obtained, amount of monthly payments, tax payments and the names of others with a financial interest in the property?

In a home fire ask the owner if he has any pets and if they were injured in the fire. In an apartment house fire, the manager should be asked: Do you know the owner or tenants, were any tenants present at the fire; what have they told you about the fire and how it started? Do you know if the owner has any other properties; has the apartment house been up for sale; are there any structural defects, any housing code violations; what is the owner's financial position; has he had any gambling losses; or any prior arrests?

Arson for profit fires are usually difficult to prove as the evidence is often largely circumstantial. It is extremely rare in this type of investigation to obtain a confession from a business owner. Many times the suspect gives a series of contradictory and inconsistent answers to key questions. The best practice is not to challenge such answers, but to prove the case in court by presenting to the jury a long list of the suspect's lies.

According to research by George Molnar and co-authors, fires for profit are usually set between midnight and dawn, often by partners in crime, using sophisticated methods to destroy non-residential property or buildings where people are not present. These partners in crime have a high level of social functioning. In contrast, fires for excitement are usually set using matches and paper or other simple methods, before midnight, by solo arsonists, with a low level of social functioning and a high frequency of mental impairment and criminal history.

Vehicle Fires

Especially when an automobile fire occurs in an isolated area at night, rather than on a heavily traveled highway in the daytime, suspect arson. Ask the owner when he purchased the car, from whom and for what price? Was there a trade-in allowance, what was the down payment, the monthly payment, are any payments overdue, and what is the total amount owing? Has he made any previous fire insurance claims? Is the car a lemon, has he had any mechanical problems? Could the car be driven at the time of the fire? Why did he have old snow tires on the front wheels when it is not a front-wheel-drive car? Is he involved in a divorce action? In other words, does he want to stop his wife from getting the car? Is he in any financial difficulties; unemployment, bills, gambling debts, divorce payments?

The driver of the car at the time of the fire should be asked for a detailed statement of all his activities for 12 hours before the fire, and for six hours after the fire.

Profile of the Compulsive Firesetter

- Usually male. May have brother or sister who is also a compulsive firesetter.
- Age 16 to 40, but may be older.
- Single or married to much older, younger or handicapped woman.
- May have singed eyebrows from recent fire, or scars and injuries from previous fires or explosions, pitted face, scars from skin grafts, missing fingers or finger tips, impaired eyesight or hearing from bomb blast or explosion.
- Poor work record, possibly paramedic, morgue attendant, security guard, gunsmith, packing house, construction or demolition worker.
- Alcohol or drug abuse.
- Schizoid loner, inadequate or antisocial personality.
- Sexual inadequacy, difficulty obtaining erection or impotence, potency is restored by setting a fire, therefore masturbates or has sexual relations at scene of fire. If he thinks he has a small penis, he may avoid using the urinal in a public restroom. Possible indecent exposure, obscene telephone calls and sexual assaults on children or adults. Males may be gay and females may be lesbians.
- Arrest record for the above sex offenses, driving under the influence of alcohol, crimes of violence including murder, impersonating a police officer or fireman, arson and bombing.
- Vehicle fire engine red with radio scanner tuned to fire department. If no vehicle, sets fires near home, work or on bus route.
- Targets may include churches, public buildings, hotels, movie theaters, apartment houses, homes, places of employment and vehicles. May set fires for excitement, but may also choose specific targets for purpose of revenge, profit or other motives.
- Increasing tension, relieved by the fire; may dream of fire the night before.
- At fire scene eager to help police, firefighters and paramedics. May need treatment for smoke inhalation. Familiar with fire-

fighting equipment, terms and radio codes, may have radio scanner. Present at too many fire scenes, late at night, fully dressed, may have alcohol on breath, may masturbate or have sexual relations in field near fire. At construction site may masturbate in portable toilet provided for workers.

- Childhood history of firesetting and fascination with fire shown by playing with matches, setting off false fire alarms, collecting firefighting equipment, pictures and books, as well as hanging around the local fire station.

- Childhood firesetting may be accompanied by cruelty to animals and by bedwetting. The bedwetting, which is significant only if accompanied by the firesetting and cruelty to animals, may continue to be a problem in adult life. The cruelty to animals may also persist, along with sadism.

- The child may have suffered serious burns in a fire that he did not set, or he may have witnessed a major fire in his own home.

- As the compulsive firesetter, may also be a compulsive bomber, he should be asked whether he has used firecrackers and cherry bombs, rockets, gun powders such as smokeless or black powder, dynamite, det cord, prima cord, plastic C4, Tovex, blasting caps, Flex X, Detaline or Detasheet. Does he reload ammunition? Has he used any chemicals or match heads to make explosives? What was his biggest explosion? What did he blow up? What does he like most: the sound, the flames or the power of the explosion? Does he get any sexual excitement? Has he ever been injured in an explosion? Has he made any pipe bombs; where did he get the idea? Did he handle explosives in the armed services or elsewhere? He may say that he has a friend who has made or used explosives when the friend is really himself. Ask questions about this friend and his actions.

- In his home he may have a radio scanner (check channel in use and channels that have been programmed); fire department codes; diaries or notes listing fires that have been set; crime scene mementos; fire equipment; books on firefighting and on explosive devices, such as *The Anarchist Cookbook* and military manuals, parcel bombs or remains of exploded bombs, accelerants, explosives and firearms; Nazi paraphernalia; pornographic pictures and magazines, as well as women's underwear.

Questioning the Compulsive Firesetter

Do not betray in word, look or gesture your disapproval of his firesetting. He is very reluctant to reveal to police or fire investigators his interest in fires, partly because he is very much aware of the strong public disapproval of arsonists. When asked whether he experiences sexual excitement at fires, he may react indignantly and say that he is not a pyromaniac, thereby revealing his knowledge of this rare disorder. If he senses that you share his interest in fires, he may talk at length about his unusual hobby.

As you question him on the features listed in the profile, he comes to realize that you are an expert on this subject. Repeating questions, rephrasing questions, moving on to other subjects and then returning once again to the issue of fires will often pay off. Do not provide him with information regarding the fire or bombing. He admits things he had previously denied, and it is easier for him to do this if you have not forcefully questioned him the first time around. Always assume that he is also a compulsive bomber and question him about explosives and explosions. Ask direct questions, such as how many bombs have you made, why do you have these manuals, why do you have this black powder, etc.

Profile of Firesetter Under Age of Seven

The following profile is from *Interviewing and Counselling Juvenile Firesetters* by Kenneth Fineman, et al., published by the United States Fire Administration.

- Poor relationship with other children: frequent jealousy; frequent breaking of other children's toys; frequent fighting; and refusal to play with other children.
- Frequently exhibits the following behavior: impulsiveness—acting before thinking; showing off; stealing; running away from home or school; cruelty to small children; cruelty to animals;

impatience; temper tantrums; nightmares; enuresis (day or night wetting); extreme mood changes- -happy to angry; feeding disorders; and accident proneness.
- Disrupted parental or home structure: parents divorced, separated or dead; lives with relative other than parents; lives in a foster home; or hospitalized for an extended period.
- Recent change in family structure: new baby; death of relative; parents recently divorced, separated; or new parent partner.
- Poor apparent relationship between mother or father or both and child: parent(s) seems hostile toward child; parent(s) criticizes child constantly or indicates how bad, dumb, ugly or unwanted the child is; lack of true parental affection; and lack of parental attention and supervision.
- Physically abused by parent(s) or guardian: beaten; burned; starved; sexually abused; or suffered unusual punishment such as confinement to a small space, such as a closet.
- Over-burdened parent.
- Physical ailment(s): obvious physical defect; frequent stomachaches; or allergies.

BOMBING

Witnesses to an explosion should be asked:
- What did you see?
- Did you see the bomber?
- Did you see anyone leaving the scene?
- Did you see anything burning before the explosion? There may have been a fuse burning.
- What was the color of the fire or smoke?
- Was there any smell before the explosion?
- Describe the sound of the explosion. Usually there is either a sharp crack (dynamite or other high explosives) or a muffled boom (black powder or gasoline).
- Was there more than one explosion?

The amateur bomber who is experimenting with explosives is often very proud of his homemade bombs and the objects he has blown up, even though the bombs may be simple, crude devices. Complimentary remarks about the technical skill of the bomb maker flatters the suspect and facilitates admission of guilt. The bomber who is making some form of social protest, for example the man who is blowing up abortion clinics, should be approached differently. Instead of talking to him about the bomb, ask him about his cause. Show some sympathy for his religious opposition to abortion and talk to him at length. Do not agree with the use of violence, but ask why he would want to use a bomb to express his point of view. The organized crime bomber may not be so ready to talk.

Every bomber should be asked questions derived from the profile of the compulsive firesetter. Does he have any explosives or time delay components in his possession? Has he made any bomb threats? Is he a member of any extreme political party, survivalist or paramilitary group?

If he senses that you, too, are an aficionado of gun-powder, he may instruct you at length on the best way to make a pipe bomb, emphasizing the necessity to oil the thread on the sections of pipe before screwing them together, in order to avoid a spark that might cost you your finger tips. He may confide his plans for building a mine field or a telephone that explodes when answered. Ask him whether he has had thoughts of making a nuclear bomb or does he know anyone who has knowledge of making bombs? He may talk about himself.

Profiles of Terrorist Bombers

Terrorists are usually men, but some groups, for example the Baader-Meinhof gang in West Germany and the Symbionese Liberation Army in the USA, included a significant number of women leaders and members. Women may be used to carry and place the bombs because they are less likely to be stopped and searched by the security forces. Profiles vary from one terrorist group to another, but in general there are:

The Leaders.

These are usually older men, from middle or upper socioeconomic class homes, with qualities of leadership, above average intelligence and a university degree or at least some university education. They are dedicated to their cause, but are no longer actively involved in bombings, assassinations or other acts of terrorism.

The Idealists.

These are people who believe in the cause for which they are risking their lives. They may also come from well-to-do homes and have university degrees or professional jobs. On the other hand, they may be dropouts who have led unstable lives. The terrorist philosophy provides an excuse for their failure to hold a job and also gives some purpose to their lives. The idealist still has some conscience, even if he uses rationalizations to excuse his criminal acts, and the interrogator can take advantage of any guilt feelings he may have for bombings that caused loss of civilian lives.

The Opportunists.

Antisocial and inadequate personalities are quick to join terrorist groups, which promise them money, glory and violence, together with protection from the police. Criminals with technical skills in the use of weapons, manufacture of bombs or knowledge of computer security systems are specially recruited by terrorists who make their acquaintance by visiting penitentiaries, sometimes as volunteers in work-release programs.

The loyalty of opportunists to the terrorist group may be minimal, and comes from fear of punishment for providing information to the police. They can be turned either by the promise of money or by the assurance that they will not be prosecuted for their crimes. An interrogator who is accustomed to dealing with informants is likely to be successful when the odds are favorable or when the person does not realize how dangerous treachery can be.

Chapter 12
CRIMINAL PROFILES

In most crime scenes the killer leaves his signature.
Roger L. Depue, FBI

The word profile refers to a side view of a person's face or a brief account of his appearance, personality and activities. If you know a man's personality, you can often predict how he will behave under varying circumstances. When a man with a particular type of personality indulges in very deviant acts, it is not unreasonable to assume that similar deviant acts may have been committed by someone with a similar personality. Thus, sadists commit acts of sadism, and it is likely, but not inevitable, that a sadistic murder was committed by a sadist.

The more deviant the crime, the more likely that criminal profiling will be of value. Commonplace criminal behavior is not usually the stuff that criminal personality profiles are made of. Nevertheless, a criminal profile based upon common methods of committing a crime may be of great practical value. An example is the profile of the behavior of the air courier who is carrying illegal drugs. Knowledge of the profile aids in identifying likely suspects.

Another example is the armed robber who, within a few weeks, hits one Shop 'n' Rob convenience store after another. Based upon reports of all the armed robberies in which he is a suspect, a profile is prepared that lists his estimated age, height, weight, ethnic group, type of weapon, getaway car, usual hours of work, locations and method of operation. No skill is required to prepare this very limited profile, which, nevertheless, serves a useful purpose.

Serial murders, bizarre murders, rape, sexual offenses against children, arson, bombing and child stealing are among the crimes that make criminal profilers jump. In these crimes, profilers have drawn upon the clinical experience of psychiatrists and psychologists who have treated or studied sadistic killers, sex offenders and compulsive firesetters.

FBI Behavioral Science
Instruction and Research Unit

The Behavioral Science Unit of the FBI Academy, under the direction of Unit Chief Roger L. Depue, has conducted pioneering research on criminal personality profiling. Members of his team include Special Agents John E. Douglas, Richard L. Ault, Robert R. Hazelwood, Kenneth V. Lanning, James Reese, Robert K. Ressler, James Horne, William Hagmaier and Ronald P. Walker. Their research is based on interviews with convicted offenders and studies of crime scene patterns. Agents in the Behavioral Science Unit have lectured to thousands of police officers across the U.S. on rape offenders, child molesters, sex murderers and organized and disorganized murderers.

Their research on crime scene and profile characteristics of organized and disorganized murderers was published in the August 1985 issue of the *FBI Law Enforcement Bulletin*. Their profiles of sex offenders have been listed in mimeographed outlines, prepared by police officers attending their classes. The authors have drawn extensively on this material, but the profiles on the above offenders do not represent the viewpoint of the FBI, and no such claim is made.

Using Profiles

Criminal profiling by the Behavioral Science Unit of the FBI Academy can provide clues to the offender's personality and behavior. Profiling does not tell you who committed the crime, it does tell you the type of person who would commit such a crime. This information is likely to be of great value when there are a number of suspects, because often it will single out a suspect. You can now concentrate all your attention on this person, and question him with great self-confidence. Many confessions have been obtained in this manner.

Analysis of the crime scene may show that two offenders, an organized murderer and a disorganized murderer, committed the crime. This crucial information about two offenders, who know each other, may lead to solution of the crime.

If there are no suspects, the profiler may be able to provide a profile of a likely suspect, including suggestions on where he lives (for example, within a short distance of where the victim's stolen car was found), where he works, his criminal record and psychiatric treatment.

The profiler can also suggest additional investigative procedures based upon his knowledge of the likely behavior of the suspect. A community meeting could be held for concerned citizens to discuss steps they should take to avoid becoming victims themselves. Witnesses and victims of crimes by the same suspect could look at people attending the meeting, through a one-way screen or on a television set. The profiler might also suggest surveillance of the murder scene or the victim's grave on the anniversary of the murder. Alternatively a voice-activated audio or video recorder could be concealed at these sites.

Profilers may also recommend measures to provoke a suspect into revealing himself, special interrogation techniques likely to be effective in obtaining a confession and advice for the prosecutor on cross-examination of the defendant. Skeptics properly demand to know the success rate of profilers, but are often too quick to emphasize the failures. They overlook the great value of profiling in helping detectives to make a thorough investigation.

Preparation of a profile is dependent on a careful examination of the crime scene, an autopsy by an experienced forensic pathologist, informed questioning of witnesses and surviving victims, information on the personality and lifestyle of the victim and a well-planned investigation for which there is no substitute. The VICAP (Violent

Criminal Apprehension Program) Crime Analysis Report form available from VICAP, FBI Academy, Quantico, VA 22135, outlines some of the information needed by profilers.

READY-MADE PROFILES

Ready-made criminal profiles, such as the ones in this book, are not as good as a specially prepared profile, based upon careful study of a particular crime by a profiler from the Behavioral Science Unit of the FBI. Requests for profiling assistance from the FBI Academy are screened by criminal profile coordinators, who are in each of the FBI's 59 field offices. Profiles should not be requested from psychiatrists or psychologists who lack street experience and the essential year-long specialized training from experienced profilers at the FBI Academy.

The profiles listed in this book suggest essential questions for surviving victims. For example, in a rape investigation the victim should be asked detailed questions on the offender's initial approach, control, attitude, assault and so on (see Chapter 8) to help the detective determine whether he is looking for a power-assurance rapist, a power-assertive rapist, an anger-retaliatory rapist, an anger-excitation rapist or an opportunist rapist.

Ready-made profiles should be modified or enlarged by the investigating detective. For example, if a rape victim reports that her assailant smelled strongly of grease, then the possibility that he worked in a garage or service station might be added to the profile. If a rape victim reported that the suspect's knife had a curve on the end, the profile might list the suspect's occupation as possibly a carpet installer or linoleum layer. If a daytime serial rapist has no clothing above his waist, he may well have removed his shirt or T-shirt because it showed the name of his employer, for example a bottling company. It may even have listed his name.

Ready-made criminal profiles also suggest questions for the suspect. In Chapter 6 the usefulness of the profile of the sadistic murderer in questioning a suspect was demonstrated. Needless to say not all the items were present in the suspect. What is surprising is the large number of items that were present both in the profile and in the suspect.

In a fire that might involve a compulsive firesetter, the suspect should be asked whether he has ever applied for employment as a firefighter or volunteer firefighter. In the investigation of sexual assault on a small boy, the detective might ask the suspect's ex-wife whether he ever asked her to wear child's clothing, ride a tricycle or shave her pubic hair. Such questions go well beyond the conventional questioning of witnesses and suspects.

Criminal profiles often include a strange assortment of items, from the suspect's choice of a car or pickup to his choice of friends, from his level of intelligence to childhood cruelty to animals, and from parental discipline to his experience in the armed services.

Some profiles, such as those on organized and disorganized murderers, are very detailed and probably will not change significantly over the years. Other profiles that are limited to a few items related mainly to the criminals' method of committing a particular crime may change as soon as the perpetrators become aware of the police tactics.

An example is provided by the successful interception of drug couriers using cars to transport drugs from Florida to other parts of the U.S. The police profile became known and the couriers changed their method of operation. Some features of such profiles cannot easily be changed, for example, nervousness, chain smoking and sweating on questioning by the police.

Information on profiles of drug couriers in airports has long been readily available in reports of legal proceedings against people arrested at airports, and has been reported in *High Times*, a monthly magazine available at most drug paraphernalia shops. Nevertheless, many couriers still draw attention to themselves by conforming to the profile. Those couriers who have learned to behave in a less conspicuous fashion, sometimes become overconfident and eventually are caught.

There is a need for care in the use of ready-made profiles. Because a suspect shows two or three items on a profile may not justify focusing the investigation on him at the expense of prompt, effective follow up of all other investigative leads. There may be no justification for submitting this suspect to prolonged questioning, which can be stressful, especially for an innocent person. Another source of error is to base the profile of a rapist on a review of all rapes in a small neighborhood. An experienced profiler reviewing police reports on these rapes, might well conclude that some of the rapes were committed by other people.

Ready-made profiles are no substitute for thorough study of the crime scene and skillful questioning of victims and witnesses. A woman is killed in her home, which has been ransacked. It might appear that the murderer is a burglar who was confronted by the victim, and he killed her. Yet an experienced detective might be able to tell at a glance that the crime scene was contrived and that a relative or acquaintance might be involved in the murder.

REFERENCES

D'Orban, P.T.: Child stealing, a typology of female offenders. *Brit J Criminol*, 16:275, 1976.

Ekman, Paul: *Telling Lies: Clues to Deceit in the Market Place, Politics and Marriage*. New York, W.W. Norton and Co., 1985.

Fuselier, G.D.: What every negotiator would like his chief to know. *FBI Law Enforcement Bull*, March 1986.

Geiselman, R.E., *et al.*: Enhancement of eyewitness memory: an empirical evaluation of the cognitive interview. *J Pol Sci & Admin*, 12:74, 1984.

Gross, Hans: *Criminal Psychology*. Boston, Little Brown and Co., 1911.

Inbau, F.E., Reid, J.E., and Buckley, J.P.: *Criminal Interrogation and Confessions*, 3rd ed. Baltimore, Williams and Wilkins, 1986.

Jones, D.P.H. and Krugman, R.D.: Can a 3-year-old child bear witness to her sexual assault and attempted murder? *Child Abuse and Neglect*, 10:253, 1986.

Jones, D.P.H. and McGraw, J.M.: Reliable and fictitious accounts of sexual abuse to children. *J Interpersonal Violence*. In press.

Kroger, W.S. and Douce, R.G.: Hypnosis in criminal investigation. *Int J Clin Exp Hypnosis*, 27:358, 1979.

Lanning, K.V.: *Child Molesters: A Behavioral Analysis*. Washington, D.C., National Center for Missing and Exploited Children, 1986.

Levin, Jack and Fox J.A.: *Mass Murder*. New York, Plenum Press, 1985.

Liebling, A.J.: *New Yorker*, 35:108, April 1959.

Link, F.C. and Foster, D.G.: *The Kinesic Interview Technique*. Riverdale, GA, Interrotec Associates, 1985.

Loftus, E.F.: *Eyewitness Testimony*. Cambridge, MA., Harvard University Press, 1979.

Macdonald, J.M.: *Armed Robbery*. Springfield, IL, Charles C. Thomas, 1975.

Macdonald, J.M.: *Burglary and Theft*. Springfield, IL, Charles C. Thomas, 1980.

Macdonald, J.M.: *Psychiatry and the Criminal*, 3rd ed. Springfield, IL, Charles C. Thomas, 1976.

Macdonald, J.M.: *The Murderer and His Victim*, 2nd ed. Springfield, IL, Charles C. Thomas, 1986.

Macdonald, J.M. and Kennedy, Jerry: *Criminal Investigation of Drug Offenses: The Narcs' Manual*. Springfield, IL, Charles C. Thomas, 1983.

McNeese, M.C. and Hebeler, J.R. The abused child. *Clin Sympos*, 29:5, 1977.

Miron, M.S. and Goldstein, A.P.: *Hostage*. Kalamazoo, MI, Behaviordelia, 1978.

Molnar, George, Keitner, Lydia, and Harwood, B.T.: A comparison of partner and solo arsonists. *J For Sci*, 29:574, 1985.

New York City Police Department: *Hostage Negotiations: Organizational and Tactical Guide*. Mimeographed. New York City Police Department, 1986.

O'Connor, J.J.: *Practical Fire and Arson Investigation*. New York, Elsevier Science Publishing Co., 1987.

Orne, M.T.: The use and misuse of hypnosis in court. *Int J Clin Exp Hypnosis*, 27:311, 1979.

Powis, David: *The Signs of Crime*. London, McGraw-Hill, 1977.

Rand, Corporation: *The Criminal Investigation Process*. Rand Corporation Technical Report, R-1776-DOJ, Santa Monica, CA, 1975.

Ressler, R.K., Burgess, A.W., Depue, R.L., Douglas, J.E., Hazelwood, R.R., and Lanning, K.V., *et al.*: Crime scene and profile characteristics of organized and disorganized murderers. *FBI Law Enforcement Bull*, August 1985.

Ressler, R.K., Burgess, A.W., Depue, R.L., Douglas, J.E., Hazelwood, R.R., and Lanning, K.V., *et al.*: Interviewing techniques for homicide investigations. *FBI Law Enforcement Bull*, August 1985.

Schlossberg, Harvey: *Sunday Times*, November 3, 1974.

Soskis, D.A., and Van Zandt, C.R.: Hostage negotiations: Law enforcement's most effective non-lethal weapon. *Behav Sci Law*, 4:423, 1986.

Yahraes, Herbert: *Why Young People Become Antisocial*. Washington, D.C., U.S. Government Printing Office, 1978.

Wolfgang, M.E.: *Patterns in Criminal Homicide*. Philadelphia, University of Pennsylvania, 1958.

INDEX